TEACHING LIBRARY SKILLS
IN SCHOOLS

Teaching Library Skills in Schools

James E. Herring MA, Dip.Lib. ALA

NFER Publishing Company

FOR VAL AND JONATHAN

ACKNOWLEDGEMENTS

The author would like to thank Mr P.H. Barker, Tutor-Librarian, De La Salle College of Education, for his help and encouragement in the preparation of this book and Mrs Ann Rabbitt, who typed out the manuscript.

Published by the NFER Publishing Company Ltd.,
Darville House, 2 Oxford Road East,
Windsor, Berks. SL4 1DF
Registered Office: The Mere, Upton Park, Slough, Berks. SL1 2DQ.
First published 1978
© James Herring
ISBN 0 85633 171 6

Typeset by Jubal Multiwrite Ltd., 66 Loampit Vale, London SE13 7SN
Printed in Great Britain by
Staples Printers, Love Lane, Rochester, Kent.
Distributed in the USA by Humanities Press Inc.,
Atlantic Highlands, New Jersey 00716 USA.

Contents

Introduction

A survey of the literature on school libraries will show that almost every aspect of this topic has been treated in some depth. An exception to this is the *teaching* of library skills. Many of the books and articles on school librarianship mention library skills only in passing, while others outline some of the skills involved but give no indication of *how* to teach these skills. It is hoped that this book will give librarians and teachers some ideas, not only on the importance of teaching library skills in schools, but also on the possible methods which might be used in actually teaching these skills.

The term 'library skills' covers a wide variety of reading skills, literary skills, alphabetic skills, number skills, etc. This book concentrates on the skills which the pupils will need in order to retrieve materials in the school library and the skills needed to effectively use the information which has been found. The skills should be developed together and become inseparable in the pupils' use of the library.

The growth of a more child-centred approach in education and the introduction of new teaching methods such as resource-based learning, discovery learning, programmed learning, team teaching, etc., has been followed by the establishment of a new kind of school library. The modern school library contains not only books but also a wide range of non-book materials for use by staff and pupils. The terms 'school resource centre', 'school library resource centre', 'school media centre' proliferate, but the term 'school library' (which is used throughout this book to cover all other terminology) is perhaps still the most accurate and helpful description.

Because of the increasing complexity of the school library, retrieval of information has become more complicated and it is no longer possible for teachers and librarians to expect pupils to find a particular piece of information merely by browsing around the shelves of the library. Also, if there is an element of closed access in relation to non-book materials, browsing may not be possible. It follows that pupils will, more than ever, need to be taught library skills if they are to use the school library to some effect. This is particularly true when pupils are doing projects on subjects which cut across the normal subject divisions. A project on POLLUTION, for example may well involve material on sociology, meteorology, chemistry, biology, geography, history etc. Haphazard retrieval of information will not produce the desired results.

A familiar objection to teaching library skills in schools is that 'library' will become another subject in the school curriculum if the pupils regard the teaching of library skills as another course to be studied. This need not be the case, if the librarian cooperates with the teachers in the school to ensure that the introduction of library skills is directly allied to the work done in the various subjects studied in school. How long it will take a librarian to teach the skills will depend on the school and the classes or groups of pupils being taught, but librarians should try to avoid extending the introductory teaching of library skills past the first term of the school year. The skills will have to be repeated, when they are needed, with individual projects for example, as long as pupils use the school library.

There appears to be no agreement on when children should be taught library skills and this may not be possible because of the differences in individual abilities amongst children. It should be possible, however, to begin teaching *some* library skills in the primary schools, perhaps at the top end, ages 8–11. If this is done, then a fuller range of library skills can be taught in the secondary school. For some less-able pupils, library skills, even in secondary schools (ages 11–16), may remain something which they find impossible to grasp and the librarian and teachers will have to attempt to teach a simpler version of the library skills outlined below. There can be no general rule on when to teach library skills, but librarians should attempt to encourage the use of library aids as early as possible in the pupils' school career.

The ideas and examples given will be most helpful to pupils either in the last year of primary school or the early years in secondary school. Such pupils, aged 10–12, will be old enough to assimilate the skills taught and will benefit from having been taught library skills at this stage of their education. Teachers and teacher-librarians whose teacher-training may not have included the study of library skills should find the following chapters helpful in their own teaching and in the work done by their pupils.

It is hoped that this book will be of use both to librarians, teacher-librarians, library school students, student-teachers and teachers. If the book can provide a wider appreciation of the need for teaching library skills and ideas on the practical teaching of these skills, then it will have served its purpose.

Chapter One

Aims and Pre-Requisites

With the growth of a more individual approach to education in our schools, the school library is increasingly being called on to play a more active role in the school curriculum. As more children use the library more often, it is essential that they have an adequate knowledge of how to exploit the potential of the school library. It follows that the pupils must be taught, in a systematic manner, the various skills and techniques they will require if they are to become competent library users.

In the past, instruction in library skills has been haphazard. At one extreme, children are taught library skills by a teacher with no training in librarianship and in an inadequately stocked school library, with no recognized classification scheme. At the other extreme a trained school librarian, running a fully catalogued, well equipped school library resource centre, teaches '. . . library usage, week after week, month after month, ad nauseam . . .'[1]

Other faults of past (and current) library instruction exist. Teachers and librarians tend to teach too much in one library lesson and the children are expected to learn much more in one library lesson than they would in a lesson on any other school subject. Also, it is too often assumed that children can understand the workings of a complicated classification scheme or a classified catalogue, despite the fact they they may have little or no previous experience of such matters.

If the children are to be taught how to use the library and then be expected to practise skills taught, the librarian[2] must plan the course of instruction with certain aims in mind. Otherwise, the instruction will be shapeless, lacking in continuity and, above all, directionless. There is little point in teaching pupils how to use the library merely as an academic exercise. Library instruction for its own sake can only

produce boredom among children and may well make the library un-
attractive to children.

In discussing the aims of teaching library skills, it is necessary to
define 'aims' as the term will be used.

The aims of teaching library skills are the purpose of such instruction, the rationale behind it. The aims should be seen in terms of user
needs rather than library provision. Thus the aims will involve what
the librarian is attempting to achieve and not the methods or the
facilities used.

The primary aim of teaching library skills should be to enable the
pupil to acquire the necessary basic skills which he/she will need to use
the library effectively. Unless this is the fundamental aim of the
librarian in his/her instruction, then any such course may be futile. The
pupils will be required to use the library effectively if the library is to
be meaningful to their educational and recreational studies. Thus a half-
hearted effort at teaching library skills will be of little use to the pupils,
as they will only gain a limited knowledge of library techniques. For
the librarian, the aim of having pupils who can use the school library is
insufficient. They must, if the exercise is to be worthwhile, be able to
use it to some effect.

Another aim of this course of instruction will be, while teaching
actual skills to children, to present the library as a place in the school
which is pleasant to work in and is a welcome alternative to the for-
mality of the classroom. The librarian will also wish to encourage the
pupils to regard the library as the prime source of information for their
studies, especially if they are involved in project work. Also, by demonstrating to pupils the range of recreational material available in the
school library, the librarian will aim at improving the attitude of the
pupils towards the library.

School libraries have a past (and in many cases, a present) which
they would like to see forgotten. The image of the school library as an
extra classroom; a storeroom; a cupboard with some books; a room
with tables, chairs and a mass of unclassified, uncatalogued books; a
place to send children who disrupt classes or have nowhere else to go
during assembly; or an unofficial common room for the sixth form, is
an image which librarians will hope to dispel, at least in the eyes of the
children.

By teaching children how to use the library effectively the librarian
can alter the image of the library and hopefully, alter the attitude of
the children towards the library. A librarian who can achieve this aim

will have solved a major problem in the successful operation of a school library. Pupils may then use the library because they *want* to, as well as because they *need* to.

When pupils use the library, their appreciation and knowledge of the workings of the classification scheme used by the library will be vital. The librarian must, therefore, include in the teaching of library skills, the aim of presenting the classification scheme as a help, easily manipulated, and not a hindrance, unbearably complicated, in using the library.

The classification scheme will have to be shown to be a series of simple, logical steps, which, if followed, will enable the pupil to tap the vast resources of the school library. Without such explanation the classification of books and non-book materials may appear intricate, unfathomable and ultimately unnecessary to the pupils.

The pupils will use the classification scheme as a means of finding information, in the form of books, fiction and non-fiction, and in non-book materials of various kinds. The librarian ought to aim at showing the pupils the variety of information, both educational and recreational, which the school library contains. A course in teaching library skills should not merely enable the pupils to manipulate the technical devices in the library (i.e. the catalogue, reference books, encyclopaedias) but ought to broaden the pupils' appreciation of the library's resources.

The pupils should be taught the existence of different types and levels of fiction; should be encouraged, by instruction as well as example, to read new fiction; and should be made aware of the library's stock of books on hobbies, sport etc. It is perhaps too often assumed that once children are shown how to use the library that they will automatically be able to appreciate what they find. This may be like teaching someone to drive a car without that person knowing where he or she wants or needs to drive to.

It is to be hoped that most modern school libraries contain or will contain not only books but also non-book materials in the shape of kits, slides, filmstrips etc. If the school library is functioning as a school library resource centre (a clumsy phrase which will hopefully disappear and be denoted by the term 'school library') and the pupils have occasion to use the non-book materials, then it will be necessary to include in the course of instruction, an introduction to the various forms of non-book materials which pupils and teachers will use.

An important aim of teaching library skills in this type of well-equipped library, will be to present the books and non-book materials as one collection of resources. Although the bookstock will remain the basis of the library, the non-book materials may become increasingly useful to the pupils and they will require the necessary skills to retrieve information from this source.

If the aim of having pupils understand and appreciate the classification scheme and the catalogue can be achieved, the aim of presenting the library as an integrated collection of resources will be made easier. An integrated catalogue in the school library will enable pupils, by using the subject index, to find information on a particular topic, both in books and non-book materials, merely by discovering the appropriate Dewey numbers for that topic.

Once the librarian decides on the aims of a course of teaching library skills, certain pre-requisites need to be fulfilled if the course is to be useful and interesting to the children.

The pupils must have a *need* for the skills they are to be taught.[3] The establishment of a school library indicates that the staff and pupils have some need of the assistance provided by a library. They need the back-up material for preparing lessons, completing projects and for recreational reading. This basic need for a library in the school provides the basis for the need for library skills.

Children may use the library without understanding the mechanics of information retrieval. They may, for instance, find books for home reading merely by browsing or by asking the librarian for 'a book about horses' or 'a ghost book'. In this manner, the *wants* of the children may be satisfied and the library is being used.

If the major aim of the librarian is to have his/her pupils use the library *effectively*, then he/she must investigate not only the *wants* (i.e. the expressed desires, recognized by the children) but also the *needs* (i.e. the unrecognized desires or requirements) of the children.

Do children, then, need to use the library effectively? If the pupils are engaged on any work which involves the retrieval of non-fiction information, a need exists for teaching library skills. If pupils use the subject approach to the library (i.e. if they seek information on a particular topic with no previous knowledge of authors or titles of books on that subject) haphazard browsing or questioning of the librarian will not suffice. Browsing will not reveal all the books which the library has on a particular topic but are not on the shelves because other pupils have borrowed them. The librarian cannot be available to answer every single subject query which the pupils will present.

Also, if pupils are encouraged to use non-book materials as well as books, they will not have the necessary retrieval skills to find information in the non-book materials, which may well be housed in a closed access system. The approach to non-book materials will almost always be by subject and the pupils, to find information, will require the necessary skills to use the catalogue.

Library skills cannot be taught in a vacuum. They should not be seen as another separate school subject as, for instance, mathematics, but must be directly related to the needs of the children. To do this, the skills must be taught in relation to subjects taught in the school. By allying lessons of library skills with classroom lessons which precede or follow the library lesson, the librarian can establish an immediate link between the library and the pupils' general educational activities in school.

Thus if pupils come to the library from, say, a history lesson, the librarian can ensure that all examples used in that particular library lesson can relate directly to what the pupils have been studying immediately prior to visiting the library. The librarian can also arrange with the history teacher that some work be set for the pupils which will include putting into practice certain library skills, as well as discovering certain historical information.

If the librarian wishes to project the image of the library as a necessary part of every subject taught in school, an important pre-requisite for teaching library skills is to involve not only pupils but teachers. The staff as a whole should be informed of the existence of the teaching of library skills; the content of the lessons and the timetable which the librarian will follow in teaching library skills. By informing and consulting the staff, the librarian not only establishes a link between library instruction and the school curriculum as a whole, but he/she may also benefit from the advice of teachers on the planning of the lessons; the examples to choose in relation to certain subjects; the different approaches which may be needed in teaching certain classes; and suggestions for pupils' work which might be done in the library once the course of library instruction has been completed.

Before a series of lessons on library skills can be taught, there must be adequate preparation by the librarian. It is important, if the teaching of library skills is to be done well, that the same preparation be given to lessons on library skills as would be given, by teachers, to any subject taught in school.

Because of lack of stress on the importance of library skills; lack of thought about the aims of teaching library skills; and lack of knowledge, by librarian, *how* to teach library skills, the instruction in library skills has often been haphazard, ill-planned and done with unfortunate haste.

The librarian must set out a plan for teaching library skills, detailing the time to be allocated for each part of the course (depending on the range of abilities of the children in different classes) and the material needed for any particular lesson, i.e. workcards, overhead projections, books, encyclopaedias etc. If the librarian feels that he/she has insufficient training in this sphere, then he/she should consult senior staff in the school for advice. It is perhaps a reflection of the lack of interest shown in school libraries by teachers in general that library instruction has been seen as something separate from the rest of the school and taught (if taught at all) in an unprofessional manner.

It should be stressed that the teaching of library skills involves the explanation of complicated library techniques, which need careful exposition, especially to the less able child. An important pre-requisite of teaching library skills should be that the instruction is done with small groups of children. It is obvious that the librarian cannot teach children the intricacies of a library catalogue if he/she must group 30 children round the school library catalogue. Where possible, the librarian ought to be able to teach one part of a class while the other part is supervized by a teacher. If the librarian is forced to attempt to teach the different library skills to the whole class, the results may well be chaotic.

A librarian who sets out to teach library skills without first examining the aims and pre-requisites of the course of instruction may well regret this lack of preparation. The result may be that the skills are taught in an unorganized manner from which neither pupils nor the librarian will benefit.

1. ROE, Ernest Teachers, librarian and children. Crosby Lockwood, 1965. Page 10.
2. 'Librarian' in this context is taken to mean either teacher-librarian or school librarian (i.e. professionally qualified librarian).
3. SAUNDERS, Helen E. The modern school library: its administration as a materials center. The Scarecrow Press, 1968. Page 28.

Chapter Two

Library Skills

Before undertaking the actual teaching of library skills, it will be useful for the librarian to ask him/herself what these skills are. If we can have as a basis for a course or series of talks on library skills, some definitions of the skills we are hoping to impart, then the teaching of these skills will be enhanced.

Library skills, in the broadest sense, may range from finding the catalogue to preparing an annotated bibliography on a particular topic. In order to progress to the more exact skills needed in using a library in the upper school or at college or university, pupils will need to be taught basic library skills, which will serve as a foundation for other skills which will be acquired later. More importantly perhaps, the basic library skills which the librarian will be teaching, will form, for most children, *all* the library skills that they will ever need.

'Basic library skills' may be defined as the skills a pupil will need to find information in the school library and to effectively use the information for an educational or recreational purpose. The information may be found in different forms, in a fiction book, a non-fiction book, a cassette, a film etc. The skills have been divided, in this chapter, into information skills and study skills and deal with the skills involved in locating and using fiction and non-fiction material.

Information skills may be divided into two overlapping categories, of locational skills[1] and evaluative skills. The librarian should study these skills carefully, because an examination of the skills will demonstrate that the process of finding information in the school library is a process which, although apparently simple, involves the pupils in a complicated number of steps, which must be taken in a definite order. If the pupil fails to recognize one of the steps or fails to follow the order of the steps, then the child will not reach the ultimate goal of finding material on the library shelves. If the librarian can break down the skills involved and foresee the difficulties which might arise, then he/she may be able to teach the skills in a more beneficial manner. Locational skills enable the child to find the guide to library use i.e. the catalogue but must be allied to evaluative skills which enable the child to evaluate the information given by the catalogue cards[2] and to proceed to the next step in the locational process.

LOCATIONAL skills will include the:
Ability to locate the card catalogue in the library.
Ability to locate the author index; an author's name; an author's name, followed by certain initials; an author's name, with certain initials followed by the title of the material (book, cassette etc.), the class number on the author card.
Ability to locate the subject index; the name of a subject; the name of that subject in relation to another subject; the class number on the subject index card.
Ability to locate the classified index; a specific class number.
Ability to locate material on the shelves, in alphabetical order (for fiction) and numerical order (non-fiction).

EVALUATIVE skills will include the:
Ability to recognize an author card for (a) fiction and (b) non-fiction[3]
Ability to differentiate between author cards with the same author but a different title.
Ability to understand the significance of the class number on an author card.
Ability to recognize a subject index card; the relationship of one subject to another subject; the significance of the class number on a subject index card.
Ability to recognize a classified card and the significance of the class number on the classified card.
Ability to recognize and understand the alphabetical and numerical sequences in the catalogue and on the shelves.
Ability to recognize the index in an encyclopaedia and its use in relation to the volumes of the encyclopaedia.

EXAMPLES

If we take an imaginary book (or film, cassette) by John Smith, with the title 'Travel by rail', we can trace the steps which the pupil must take and the locational and evaluative skills involved.

The pupil has to find the catalogue and the author index; the name SMITH (there may be more than one SMITH); the name SMITH, John. The pupil then has to recognize that the first card with this name is not necessarily the card being looked for. The card must have the title 'Travel by rail' and the pupil will have to recognize and follow the alphabetical sequence of titles on the cards with the name SMITH, John.

The author card will (in this case) have a class number and the pupil must be able to recognize the class number and understand how it is used. For this book or cassette the class number would be 385 SMI (the Dewey number followed by the first three letters of the author's name). The pupil must then realize that the class number indicates that the book is shelved at 385 SMI.

If the same pupil was doing a project on RAILWAYS he/she would have to find the subject index and find, in alphabetical order, the subject RAILWAYS. When this card is found the pupil may find that a decision is involved. The card may read RAILWAYS: ENGINEERING and may be followed by another card which reads RAILWAYS: TRAVEL. The pupil must decide if he/she needs either or both of these cards.

The subject index in this case provides the pupil with the subject RAILWAYS in relation to two other subjects ENGINEERING and TRAVEL. The pupil is also given two class numbers, so that the cards will read.

| RAILWAYS: ENGINEERING | 625.1 |
| RAILWAYS: TRAVEL | 385 |

The significance of the class number must be understood if the pupil is to locate the material. The class number tells the pupil that all the material on a particular topic of shelved at the number given.

The pupil then has two choices, which must be appreciated. He/she can either go directly to the shelves 625.1 or 385 (or both) and find the material which is in the library, at that particular time or the pupil can consult the classified index under the class number(s) to find out *all* the material which the library has, both on the shelves or on loan to staff or pupils.

In the classified index the pupil will find the cards in numerical order and must understand that when he/she reaches the number 385, all the material on that subject will be listed under that number.

Having consulted the catalogue, the pupil can then proceed to the shelves with (a) the class number 385 SMI or (b) the class numbers 385 and 625.1 or (c) a list of all the material which the library has on the subject RAILWAYS: TRAVEL. The fiction shelves will be arranged alphabetically and the non-fiction shelves numerically. The pupil has to understand the process of locating 385 SMI. That is, he/she must follow the numerical sequence to 385 and then the alphabetical sequence within that number to 385 SMI.

If the pupil is seeking only a short note on RAILWAYS, he/she may consult the encyclopaedias. The pupil must then appreciate the initial organization of the encyclopaedias (alphabetical by subject) and also the relationship of the index to the other volumes.

One reason for the lack of proper attention which has been paid to teaching library skills in the past may be that those teaching the skills have not appreciated the apparent intricacies of the locational process in libraries. By completing a task analysis on the finding of a piece of information in a library, the librarian can so direct his planning of the teaching of the skills, that it will take into account the need for careful, varied and often repeated explanation of the different skills. Librarians should not assume that pupils will be able to complete the locational process, or any part of it, without being shown how and why that process exists.

Having taught information skills to pupils, the librarian will wish to see the pupils using the materials they have found. The effective use of the information located will ensure that the pupils gain some benefit from their library experience, but to ensure effective use of the material, the librarian and the teacher will have to ally study skills or comprehension skills to the information skills already acquired by pupils.

Study skills are less well defined than information skills but generally constitute the skills required to extract information and ideas from what is being read and to transmit the information and ideas in a written form or into new knowledge which is appreciated by the pupil and can be stored for further use. In short, study skills enable pupils to learn from what they read or look at or listen to. Most of the study skills will have been taught to pupils in primary (5–11 years) grades but in most cases, will need to be re-taught in the secondary school. For the librarian, who may have no professional training in teaching such skills, an outline of what study skills entail may be useful. It must be stressed, however, that the librarian should always approach the teaching of study skills in cooperation with the teacher and with the librarian playing a secondary role.

Study skills or comprehension skills[3] include the ability to:

Appreciate the purpose for reading (or viewing or listening);
Set questions which can be answered from the text;
Use skimming skills or scanning skills to identify the relevant facts and ideas in the text;
Make useful notes from the text, arranging disparate facts and ideas taken from the text;
Evaluate the information in the text and draw conclusions from the text;
Present the information gained in an organized, written form;
Use the technical skills to operate audio-visual hardware;
Locate and select information in non-book materials;
Use listening skills and viewing skills.

Thus if a pupil approaches a passage in a book or encyclopaedia in order to gain information on, for example, VICTORIAN TOWNS, there must firstly be a definite purpose for reading the passage. This purpose, to find information for the project on TOWNS, must be appreciated by the pupil. The pupil must then know how to effectively extract the information needed. By setting questions which must be answered from the text, the pupil can give some structure to the information gained. For example, the pupil might set the question: what kinds of shops were available to Victorian city-dwellers?

Skimming skills or recognition skills enable the pupil to read a passage and recognize the details which are relevant to the questions set. Effective use of these skills will enable the pupils to read selectively, choosing information, in this case, on housing in towns but quickly reading over a passage on transport, which might be the topic for another group in the class.

Having recognized the relevant information, the pupil then has to be able to take notes from the passage. The notes should be so arranged as to bring together facts and ideas from the passage. Thus the pupil will have to collect together all the facts on housing which may appear at different points in a chapter on VICTORIAN TOWNS.

A more difficult skill to acquire than the arrangement of information, is the evaluation of what is being read. The pupil must be able to judge what is fact and what is opinion, what is relevant to the topic being studied, what should be noted down and what can be ignored. The evaluation of information from different sources is also important. The information given on living conditions in tenements may be slightly different in a book and an encyclopaedia. The pupil may find, by evaluating the information, that the statistics in the book are taken from London and in the encyclopaedia from Glasgow, which may account for the difference. Another aspect of evaluation is that the pupil must relate what is being read to the knowledge of the topic he/she has already acquired, perhaps from a filmstrip on TOWNS shown by the teacher in classroom. Following on from this, the pupil should be able to isolate the relevant facts and ideas in the passage, to determine the relationships between the facts and ideas and to draw some conclusions from the information. Thus from a chapter on VICTORIAN TOWNS the pupil may be able to judge the causes of the slum conditions which existed in cities.

When a passage or chapter has been read, the pupil will be expected to present the information in a written form. The ability to write about what has been read, using paragraphs which relate to each other and follow a logical order, is an important skill. Otherwise, the pupil's written report becomes a mass of unrelated facts.

Until recently, almost all the information sought by pupils in school libraries was contained in printed form, and books, articles and reference works seem likely to continue to be the main carriers of information. The development of audio-visual media and its use in schools means that the pupils will increasingly be faced with the task of extracting information from non-book materials. The study skills discussed above will still be relevant but certain other skills will be needed for the effective use of the new materials.

The operation of hardware and software by pupils will involve technical skills previously unknown to pupils. These skills involve working slide projectors, threading filmstrips, operating cassette recorders etc. Allied to these skills will be the skills needed to locate information in non-book materials. Such skills include the location of an index in a filmstrip with notes, the contents list in a set of slides or passages on related topics in a cassette.

The selection of relevant information from a filmstrip or cassette may be more difficult than from a book and pupils will have to be taught how to use skimming skills in relation to non-book materials. The setting of questions to be answered will be more important with audio-visual media because of the need for pupils to translate visual images into a written form. Also, listening to a cassette or viewing a filmstrip will require different levels of concentration from pupils and these skills will have to be developed if the pupils are to benefit from using non-book materials.

Information skills and study skills are inseparable in library use by pupils. The acquisition of only one of the types of skill will prove a great drawback to the pupil in the library. The skills should, therefore, be related when they are taught. For example, the headings which are looked up in the subject index may form the headings used in the notes made by the pupil. Thus a pupil writing an essay on VICTORIAN TOWNS may find such headings as FACTORIES, INDUSTRY, POVERTY, SLUMS, TENEMENTS in the subject index then use these headings as the structure for his/her essay.

1. POLETTE, Nancy: Developing methods of inquiry, Scarecrow Press, 1973. p.103
2. It is being assumed that the school library catalogue will consist of an author index, a classified index and a subject index. Some schools may have other types of catalogue, a dictionary catalogue for example, but the skills involved will not be different.
3. A useful guide to these skills is given in WINKWORTH, F.V.: User education in schools. This is a British Library Report which includes a table listing the different library skills. Also relevant is OPEN UNIVERSITY. PE261: Reading Development, units 3 and 4, which explains comprehension skills (study skills) in some depth.

Chapter Three

The Librarian and the Teacher

The teaching of library skills will affect the pupils' use of the library in relation to the subjects they study in school and in relation to their recreational reading and activities. If the library is part of the school, part of each subject, then it follows that the librarian is also (potentially) part of each subject department, almost an extra member of staff for each subject. Thus the librarian cannot teach library skills without contributions from the teachers of the various subjects. The relationship between the librarian and the teachers in a school will differ from school to school but if the librarian intends to teach library skills successfully and then to see the skills being put into effect, there are certain steps which will have to be taken.

The librarian must not be isolated from the rest of the staff; must publicize the work done in the library: must discuss with each subject department how the library can or should affect that department; must explain the need for teaching library skills and ask for advice and co-operation in the teaching of the skills; must discuss selection and evaluation procedures with the teachers. In short, the librarian has to take the library to the staff and convince them that without the existence of the school library, the educational and recreational needs of the pupils would be unfulfilled.

If we take the teaching of library skills as a focal point of the librarian's work, it should be obvious that the librarian cannot avoid contact with the other staff. Because library skills affect the teachers' work in the school, the librarian must maintain constant contacts with the whole staff. In many cases, the most valuable work done by the librarian vis-a-vis the staff, will be done in the staffroom or common room. It is here that the librarian can make the informal contacts which

will lead to more formal discussions. Much will depend on the persona-
lity of the librarian, whose task is to convince the teachers of the need
for teaching library skills and to show them that some positive benefit
will occur *for teachers* if library skills are developed.

The librarian therefore, must be a full member of staff, attending
functions and meetings and generally becoming involved in some of the
extra-curricular activities of the school, from the staff five-a-side football team to the school debating society. Only by doing this, by becoming, in the teachers' eyes, another teacher, can the librarian become accepted as a respected member of staff. Sitting isolated in the library,
the librarian will only create ill-feeling and further isolation from the
staff. In the staffroom, the librarian can find out the attitudes of the
teachers to the school library. Do they think the library has a positive
role to play in the school? Could it be improved? Could there be more
books and non-book materials on geography? Could part of a history
course be taught in one part of the library? From such contact with
teachers, the librarian will find out which members of staff are most ap-
proachable, most interested in libraries and most amenable to suggestions. The librarian can discover the particular interests, curricular and
otherwise, of certain members of staff and can later send them any new
material relevant to their interest, which comes into the library. This
type of personal help builds confidence in the librarian. An example of
this type of direct, unrequested help would be the librarian being told
of a new book on remedial teaching by one of the Schools Library Service staff, and borrowing that book for a remedial teacher in the school.

It is those members of staff who show some awareness of the school
library and a wish for its greater exploitation, that the librarian should
work with first. Only by a practical demonstration of the library's help
to some teachers will the librarian impress those other teachers who
seem less interested in the library. The initial stages will involve discussion in the staffroom. 'What was the library like when you were at
school?' the librarian might ask some teachers. 'What was it like at
college?' or 'Don't you think the library could be better used by all of
us?'. Once the librarian starts the teachers discussing the library and
library matters, he/she has established an interest in the library amongst
the staff. This interest should be built upon.

The next step for the librarian is to publicize the actual and possible
work done in the library, by the librarian, by the teacher and by the
pupils. The work done by the librarian may not be immediately obvious
to the teachers, apart from specifically professional tasks such as cata-

loguing and classification and routine tasks such as shelving, filing etc. The librarian has to widen the appreciation of his/her own job (and that of the library) by discussing with colleagues ways in which the librarian can become more fully integrated into the life of the school. For example, an informal chat with a history teacher might reveal that one of the sixth form is working on a paper on the rise of Nazism in Germany. The librarian may then suggest that there is some material in the school library on this topic, but for this level of student, material could be borrowed from the Schools Library Service or the Public Library. This may be a service of which the teacher is unaware. Following on from this, the librarian may borrow the material, pass it on to the sixth former but discover that the sixth former has little idea of how to find information on this topic in the school library. 'Do the sixth form need some help in developing library skills?' the librarian might ask the history teacher. Discussions with the history teacher (and others) could lead to the development of a short course on information retrieval for the sixth form, which would be preceded by a visit to the library by the history teacher to discover the material available on historical topics and how this material could be used to help the sixth form improve their use of the library.

The librarian's bibliographical skills should also be made available to staff. The school library should be the information storehouse of the school, so that if the headmaster wants to know the address of the Schools Council or the science teacher wants to find out the publisher of a biology book, they will ask or telephone the librarian. By gradually demonstrating that the skills of the librarian are applicable to all departments, the librarian can make the library the place which staff will first think of when information is required.

The librarian's work with the pupils in the library is the closest link between the librarian and the teacher. Involvement with pupils, at all levels, means that the librarian will have experiences that can be shared directly with the teachers. Thus the librarian will meet the same difficulties with some pupils, who behave badly in class and in the library. Other pupils will be avid readers of fiction, known to teachers and librarians, while yet other pupils will have potential which needs to be encouraged in class and in the library.

What the librarian does to help pupils in the library must be communicated to the teachers, who, because of timetable pressures may not have the opportunity to visit the library often. An example of this might be a group of pupils doing a project (see also chapter 12) on

TOWNS with the geography teacher. The librarian will have been involved with the pupils perhaps in their use of the catalogue, by asking the pupils to think of possible subject headings which they could look up in the subject index for information on TOWNS. In the discussions with the pupils, the librarian might have found that the pupils, by themselves, had discovered that by thinking of the different aspects of a TOWN, they had located information on BUILDINGS, ELECTRICITY, GAS, LOCAL GOVERNMENT, MARKETS, SEWERS, SHOPS, TOWN PLANNING, TRAFFIC, WATERWORKS, as well as information from general history, geography and science books. The geography teacher may not be aware of the potential benefit to be gained from greater library use for his classes. It is up to the librarian, by advertising the use of the library, to remedy such a situation.

With this same teacher, the librarian might suggest that with the next class project or the next time TOWNS is taken as a project, they try to improve the pupils' appreciation of the topic (and of the library) by better classroom/library links. This could take the form of the teacher informing the librarian when the topic is to be covered, so that the librarian can prepare suitable materials for the project. This might involve borrowing books and non-book materials from the Schools Library Service or Area Resource Centre. Does the geography teacher realise that this borrowing facility, which could treble the materials available to pupils, exists?

Another advantage of forward planning for a project, is that the librarian and the teacher can discuss the methods used in teaching the project. This does not imply that the librarian will be examining the classroom teaching done by the teacher but will involve discussion about the library skills needed for this type of work. Does the teacher wish the librarian to give a short explanation, with examples relevant to the topic, of what library skills will be involved in finding material for the project? How much should the pupils be expected to find their own material and how much help should they be given by the librarian? Will the librarian or teacher or both be involved in explaining or re-introducing the study skills involved in the project? Does the teacher wish to borrow library materials for a classroom introduction to the project — a videotape on public utilities in TOWNS, for example? Does the school library house this material or will it be borrowed from the Schools Library Service?

This type of planning between the librarian and a particular teacher can only be done through personal, verbal contact with the teacher. A notice on the staffroom board telling of the possibilities of borrowing material from other libraries may well be lost between the staff–pupil hockey match and the new charges for coffee and tea. The librarian, in advertising what can be done in the library for and with pupils, is like a door-to-door salesman. On the one hand, he/she can put a leaflet in the pigeonholes in the staffroom, but this will be similar to a sales leaflet through the letter-box. It is not effective because it is impersonal and there is too much opposition from similar types of advertising. The librarian should talk to individual members of staff to ensure any response, should offer definite suggestions which will be seen as helpful by teachers. The process of personally contacting all members of staff will be a gradual one and not always successful, but by demonstrating the library's potential to a number of teachers, the librarian can go to establish the library in the minds of the staff as a whole. Help given for one project or course will lead to requests from other teachers for similar help. Thus if the librarian borrows a videotape on THE GROWTH OF TOWNS for a geography teacher, the history teacher may subsequently ask to see the same videotape or ask whether a videotape on TOWNS IN THE INDUSTRIAL REVOLUTION is available.

The growth of such interest in the library services within the school will start in the staffroom during lunchtimes or intervals. The librarian should be aware of the advantages of such informal discussions. Talking to one teacher in a group of teachers can lead to interest from the group as a whole. This if the librarian borrows the videotape THE GROWTH OF TOWNS, it is much better if the videotape is taken to the staffroom and given to the geography teacher, *in full view of other teachers*, rather than leaving a note for the geography teacher to collect it from the library.

More formal contacts will be made on a departmental level, usually through heads of department. If the librarian can convince the head of department that the library can make a positive contribution to the teaching of the subject, certain decisions affecting the library and the department can be made. For example, if the head of Home Economics finds that there is much material available in and through the school library, on such subjects as DIETETICS, FABRICS, NEEDLEWORK, FOOD SCIENCE etc., more work may be done by that department in cooperation with the librarian. Such work would include the teaching or re-teaching of library skills which the pupils would need when seeking material on home economics topics. The librarian may subsequently be involved in meetings of the Home Economics department. Such meetings will be valuable for the librarian and any opportunity to attend departmental meetings should not be missed. At the meetings the librarian will gain an insight into the courses taught by the department and will be given the opportunity to suggest ways in which the library and the department could liaise. One method of ensuring continuing links with all departments is for each department to have one member responsible for library matters, which would include suggestions for the purchase of books and non-book materials, arranging for classes to use the library for project work and helping with subject displays in the library. The librarian could provide reviews of books and non-book materials on home economics, publishers' catalogues and information on what can be borrowed from outside sources.

The promotion of fiction is an important feature of the librarian's work in the school (see chapter 7) and the involvement of teachers is vital. Traditionally, children's fiction has been seen as the prerogative of the librarian and the English department but this attitude to fiction, which departmentalizes children's literature, deprives the librarian of the help and advice which other teachers can give. The librarian may be able, in a few cases, to ask members of staff not in the English department, but who are known to the librarian as readers of (adult) fiction, to read a children's novel and give an opinion on it. Thus if Mr Ferguson, the head of geography has enjoyed 'The Machine Gunners' pupils may be more impressed than if an English teacher had read it. This approach may appear to be naive, but in the author's own experience, it has been successful on a limited number of occasions.

The English department will be directly involved with the fiction read by the pupils and the librarian must maintain close contacts with the department to ensure that he/she knows what is being taught, how it is being taught and to what extent the library will be involved in the educational as well as recreational aspects of fiction-reading by the pupils.

An example of this is the reading list, either class-list or year-list. Discussions between the librarian and the English teachers are important concerning the content of the lists. Can the librarian make suggestions for additions to the lists if suitable new books arrive in the library? If a pupil wishes to read 'Thunder and lightnings' by Jan Mark, but the book is not on the list, can the pupil use the book (with the teacher's permission) as his/her class reader? The librarian will be able to produce lists for the teacher which deal with fiction for particular groups such as slow readers, teenage girls or very intelligent first year pupils. Also, if the librarian can find out from the English department what is being taught not only this term, but *next term*, it may be possible to gather material together in the library for use with a particular group or class and to produce a reading list for that group.

In chapter 2, it was stated that library skills could not be taught in a vacuum but should be taught in relation to school subjects. In almost all aspects of teaching library skills, the librarian will require the cooperation and help of the teachers. The examples used by the librarian should relate to work being done by the pupils in school, therefore the librarian must discuss with the teachers which topics might be used as examples. Before such arrangements are made, it is important that the staff know what is included in the teaching of library skills. Some teachers may be suspicious of 'teaching' being done by a non-teacher. To allay such fears, the librarian should publicize what the content of the library skills programme will be. The content can be given in a written plan or in a verbal explanation.

A written plan could be drawn up and given to each member of staff. The librarian would describe the essentials of the course, classification, the catalogue, reference material, fiction, non-book materials etc. and suggest ways in which the teaching of the various skills could be linked with subjects taught in class. The plan should be as brief as possible and give concrete examples, perhaps relating catalogue use to a geography lesson on FARMING IN GREAT BRITAIN.

A plan given verbally would have more impact. A talk by the librarian to the staff as a whole would have to be arranged through the principal or headmaster. In this talk, the librarian can explain in more detail what skills he/she feels the pupils ought to acquire. This will also be an opportunity to explain the library system to members of staff who might not be fully aware of how the system operated. The organization and retrieval of non-book materials in the school library may be an aspect of libraries not previously experienced by some teachers. Teaching the teachers about the school library is the most delicate aspect of demonstrating the need for teaching library skills and the librarian will have to avoid offending those teachers who (a) know how to use the library effectively or (b) do not know how to use the library effectively but do not wish to be shown by the librarian. An explanation of what the pupils would be expected to learn could be followed by visits to the library by members of different departments, perhaps on a rota basis. These visits, the librarian can explain in the talk, would take the form of discussions and suggestions from librarian and teachers about the library system. The talk to the staff should be carefully worded. It should not be a lecture on library skills but should contain an appeal for cooperation and help from the teachers. The teaching or re-teaching of study skills will be an important element of the pupils work in the library and the librarian should make it clear that he/she cannot hope to ensure that the pupils adequately profit from their library use unless they know how to use the information they find. The librarian's talk will be successful if the teachers feel that they are being asked to add their professional expertise to the professional skills and knowledge of the librarian and that the teaching of their own subject will be enhanced by a greater application of library skills by themselves and their pupils.

If we return to the geography teacher and the project on TOWNS, we can examine how the librarian could follow up the talk given to the whole staff, in discussions with one member of staff. If the project is being taught when the pupils are being introduced to library skills, examples from the project can be used by the librarian and the teacher in explaining the use of reference material. The teacher may take an atlas, a gazetteer and an encyclopaedia to the classroom and explain how the different reference tools are used. When the pupils are in the library, the librarian, when discussing reference works, can repeat one teacher's introduction and relate it to other reference works. Thus if the topic is TOWN PLANNING, the librarian might point out that WHITAKER'S ALMANAC is a useful source for general information on this topic.

In relation to study skills, the teacher may explain to the pupils how to read a passage, for example on LOCAL GOVERNMENT, and by using skimming skills, pick out the relevant information on the structure of the District Council. The librarian and the teacher will have to decide whether the study skills need to be re-explained in the library and whether the librarian or the teacher or both should be involved. The librarian may not have the professional background to teach study skills in depth, but he/she may be able, under the teacher's guidance, to reinforce what the teacher has taught, demonstrating to a group how they should, for example, set themselves questions to answer before taking notes from a passage in an encyclopaedia on PUBLIC UTILITIES.

The selection and evaluation of materials which the pupils will use in the library, will be an important aspect of librarian-teacher relations closely linked to teaching library skills. There will have to be an adequate amount of material available to support the teaching programme in the school and the books and non-book materials chosen will have to be relevant to the needs of the individual subjects as well as to the needs of the school as a whole. Criteria for selection and evaluation of books and non-book materials are fully discussed by Beswick[1] and need not be listed here. The effectiveness of the library material (and of the library itself) will depend on how closely the material selected is suited to what is being taught in the school. Because of the delay in ordering and processing books and non-book materials, forward planning for the selection and evaluation of material is necessary for librarian and teacher. If this planning is not done, a situation may arise where the teacher sends a group to the library to work on a topic but there is little material available. To avoid such occasions the librarian will have to find out the content of the various courses in the school and discuss with each department any special needs they might have during the next term.

If, as has been suggested, each department has one member of staff responsible for liaising with the library, the librarian can provide information on new material in the form of publishers' catalogues and leaflets, book reviews, articles on non-book materials, as well as keeping in the library periodicals such as the School Librarian, Signal, Children's Literature in Education, Junior Bookshelf. This may be seen as the traditional role of the librarian in the selection of material. Information of this nature, however, may suffer the same fate as the salesman's leaflet. The availability of reviews, articles etc. does not ensure a response from a teacher in a particular department. A review of a book on STUDYING THE LOCAL ENVIRONMENT may not make it clear whether the book is useful, *in a particular school*, for pupils studying biology or geography, or both. What will interest the teacher and what the teacher wishes to see (like the salesman's customer) is the material itself, whether book, film or cassette.

Thus the librarian should try, as much as possible, to borrow materials from the Schools Library Service or other sources, show them to the teachers and then decide whether to buy them.[2] This is particularly true of non-book materials. A filmstrip on THE LOCAL ENVIRONMENT may suit one school but not another. The librarian may be able to borrow it from the Area Resource Centre before a decision on its purchase is made. Non-fiction books for use with certain groups of pupils, may have to be inspected, by the remedial teacher for example, to ensure that the books are suitable for remedial pupils, *in that school*. As the librarian selects material for the library, over a period of time he/she will come to know better the requirements and preferences of individual teachers. Eventually a system may emerge whereby when any new course is introduced, the librarian will be consulted as to the availability and quality of materials for the course.

The relationship between the librarian and the other school staff, from principal to newly-trained teacher, will be a successful one if the librarian is prepared to 'sell' the library to the staff. The librarian must try to be constantly available; to always have some material available on a requested topic; to always appear helpful and polite; to have an excellent memory, so that he/she can remember every request made by pupil and teacher alike; to successfully promote fiction amongst all pupils; to teach library skills with the effect of producing pupils who can use the library to improve their educational performance. In short, the librarian will be expected to be librarian, teacher, counsellor, organizer, administrator and information officer rolled into one. With a good librarian—teacher relationship, the librarian may be able to shed some of the load.

1. BESWICK, Norman: Resource-based learning. Heinemann, 1977.
2. An example of this is the service offered by the Educational Resource Service to teachers and librarians in schools in the Lanark Division of Strathclyde Region. School librarians can visit the Bell Educational Resource Centre to borrow books and non-book materials and view displays of books, kits, play sets, tapes, slides etc. This facility (used by the author) provided an excellent back-up service for the school librarian and teachers.

Chapter Four

Introducing the Library
and the Librarian

There is no set formula for teaching library skills. All school librarians will be teaching the same skills, but they will be teaching them for use in many different types, sizes and standards of school library. The following chapters represent some ideas and suggestions for teaching library skills. Each librarian will, of necessity, have to adapt these ideas to his/her own shool library and use examples from the library in which the skills are to be taught.

Some parts of the teaching may be accompanied by handouts to children or slides showing examples in the school library but as these will be unique to each school library,[1] no examples are given here. In some cases, with classification for example, an overhead projector may well be the ideal means of most easily communicating the ideas behind the subject, but to include suggestions for overhead projections would be confusing and not helpful.

The period of time taken by each librarian to teach the skills needed will also vary from school to school and, indeed, from class to class. There are, therefore, no suggestions as to how much the librarian should attempt to teach in one lesson or library period. Librarians may well discover that, having split a class into groups, one group will understand a particular skill immediately and apply it, while another group may have difficulties. The practical organization of groups and classes has been left to the individual librarian.

A basic part of any course on library skills will be the introduction to the library and the librarian. This is especially true of pupils who are in their first year at a new school. It is worthwhile spending at least one whole session or period in explaining to the children the basic facts about the library.

Before this, the librarian must introduce her/himself. It is important especially in larger schools, that pupils know who the librarian is and what his/her name is. If the librarian is a full-time school librarian, he/she will explain to the children the role of the librarian, emphasizing that the librarian is primarily there to help the children, not only with school work but also with recreational activities. To a great extent, the image of the librarian which the children perceive will influence their attitude to the school library. If the full-time school librarian can convince the pupils that the librarian has the same authority as a teacher, but is something more than a teacher, then the pupils will react favourably. Although the respect of the pupils will be gained over a period of time, the first impression of the librarian will be important to children, especially if they have not encountered a school librarian before.

The above points are equally important for teacher-librarians. In their role as teachers they may not come into contact with all the pupils involved in library instruction, so it is important that children recognize the name of that teacher, not only as, for example, the history teacher, but also as the school librarian (something *more* than a teacher). The teacher-librarian should stress that he/she is able to help the children in a different way from that of a class teacher. For instance, it could be stressed that as a librarian the teacher-librarian can help pupils to find information on any school subject for projects done in school. In this way the pupils can see that the teacher librarian is someone outside the strictly departmentalized structure of the school and this can be a distinct advantage for the teacher-librarian.

Having introduced him/herself the librarian can then show the children the various aspects of the library. It is worthwhile taking the children (in groups perhaps) on a short tour of the library, showing them the physical lay-out. The pupils then immediately know where the encyclopaedias are kept, where the reference section is, what the catalogue looks like and where to return or take out library books. This may appear to be superfluous information but the librarian should not assume that if a child is told to consult an encyclopaedia, the child, without previous help, will be able to find the encyclopaedias.

The next step the librarian will take is to explain the functioning of the library, i.e. how a book can be borrowed, for how long it can be borrowed, whether a ticket is needed for each book, whether there are fines for books returned late, whether books can be requested, when the library is open and whether there are certain days on which certain years in the school can use the library.[1]

These might be called 'library rules'. In the past, in many libraries, it seems that the 'rules' have consisted of a series of 'do not's' which point out to the children all the negative aspects of using the school library, e.g. do not come into the library with dirty hands; do not run in the library or (even worse) do not talk in the library.

As the children's first image of the library and the librarian may well be this introduction to the library, it seems obvious that if the children are bombarded with a list of actions they must not take in the library, then their image of the library will be a negative one. The library will be a place, not for doing something positive but for *not* doing something negative.

The approach to this part of teaching library skills (and the children's attitude to and behaviour in the library will be a fundamental part of their library skills) is vital. If the librarian adopts a positive attitude, then the children will respond. The librarian, for example, can explain that when a book is to be borrowed, the pupil will select the book, take it to the counter, hand over the library ticket (on which the pupil should write his/her own name) and have the book stamped. The pupil then has the book for two weeks and returns it.

At this point, the librarian can emphasize that if the pupil does not return the book on time, then either his/her form teacher will be told and the pupil will have to pay a fine. On the other hand, the librarian can explain to the children that they should return their books on time because other pupils will be waiting for that book and that they themselves would not want to wait for a book which another pupil had not returned on time. This approach is more positive. Fines in a school library can be counter-productive. The revenue they bring in is negligible and they do not ensure a better return of books on time. Instead they represent a totally unnecessary threat to the pupil which may cause that pupil to see only the negative aspects of the library or to avoid taking books out in fear that they may be returned late.

On the question of discipline and behaviour in the library, the librarian should stress what *is* allowed in the library. The pupils should be allowed to talk without causing undue noise unless the librarian or another teacher is speaking to them. 'Silence' notices in school libraries are anachronisms. It should be obvious to any teacher or librarian that pupils may act somewhat differently in a library than in a classroom, primarily because pupils may be facing each other across tables or walking round the shelves. More importantly, there is no *need* for complete silence in a school library.

If the librarian explains to the pupils that, in the library, they will be expected to behave as they behave in the classroom, the children will see this as a normal part of school life. What the librarian must show the pupils is that, in the library, they are being given slightly more freedom (to walk round the shelves, to discuss books) than normal. The library can, therefore, become a place in the school which pupils see as more open than the classroom and the pupils have a positive image of the library in this respect.

This does not mean that the librarian is willing to allow pupils to tear the books up or to shout at each other across the library, but there is no point in overstressing aspects of indiscipline in the library. The pupils should see the library as a place of enjoyment and not a privileged shelter of books and resources which they are allowed to use only if they promise to behave.

Over-zealous enforcement of rules has been a feature of too many school libraries. In his book 'The teacher-librarian' Ernest Grimshaw falls into the trap of presenting a negative image of the school library. 'Library rules. Two should be sufficient. 1. Silence. 2. Care of books and furniture . . .'[2] In other words, 1. Do not write on the walls 2. Obey all the rules!

Grimshaw goes on to suggest that there might be a list in the library of 'Library Don'ts', which include 'Don't wet the fingers before turning pages'[3] He goes on to state that 'The art teacher might make a series of posters to illustrate the above points, (library don'ts).[4]

No teacher in a classroom would ever consider putting notices on the wall explaining how children should behave or how they should treat books. Because pupils are in a library does not mean that they will instantly lose all control over their own discipline. We must remember that Grimshaw wrote his book in 1952 and that attitudes to children in schools have changed. Unfortunately librarians in some schools may not have moved away from the Grimshaw model as much as is desirable. Teacher-librarians especially should ask themselves whether they teach pupils in a more rigid fashion in the library than they do in the classroom.

If pupils misbehave or mistreat books in the library, the librarian should deal with these incidents as they occur, as would happen in a classroom. To spend time explaining school standards of behaviour to pupils who already know what these standards are, seems ludicrous.

The introduction of the librarian and the library to pupils is a part of teaching library skills which the librarian must plan carefully. The approach of the librarian to this introduction may well shape the attitude which the pupils take to the subsequent talks and sessions on library skills.

1. SMITH, Barbara G. 'How do I join, please?'. School Librarian, Vol. 24 No. 2, June 1976, 109—111. This article is a helpful guide on explaining the basics of the library by verbal and audio-visual methods.
2. GRIMSHAW, Ernest. 'The teacher-librarian'. Arnold, 1952. Page 1. 106.
3. *Ibid*. Page 1. 115.
4. *Ibid*. Page 1. 115.

Chapter Five

Fiction and Non-Fiction

One of the first hurdles to be crossed in teaching library skills is to explain to pupils the difference between fiction and non-fiction. Some pupils will undoubtedly already know the difference, while for others, the distinction may be difficult to grasp. It may be useful to explain the two concepts in separate visits to the library in order to avoid confusion.

In teaching the concept of fiction, the librarian should include in the explanation several examples of fiction books. Pupils can be shown what fiction books tend to look like. The covers are good examples, as they usually depict the setting of the story or an incident in the tale. Also, fiction books are generally smaller than non-fiction books.

It should first be explained to the pupils that fiction books contain stories which are not true events, but made up. A useful mnemonic might be 'F for fiction, F for fairy-tale' which stresses the idea that fiction consists of imaginary tales. Most pupils will have read works of fiction and it is worthwhile asking for examples of books and authors of fiction from children. Examples of works of fiction which have been serialized on television are also useful. This enables the librarian to repeat what has already been said and to see whether some of the children may not have grasped the concept.

Having explained what fiction is, the librarian should not, as has perhaps been done in the past, stop at this point. The librarian is trying not only to enable the pupils to understand the abstract concept of fiction but is also trying to encourage the children to read fiction books in the library. Thus having explained the product, the librarian now has to sell it.

Throughout the teaching of library skills the librarian will be attempting to show the pupils that the library and the books and resources therein is not something unconnected with their school life or home life, but in many ways is closer to their life outside school than any other part of their school experience. In 'selling' fiction to pupils, the librarian should attempt to demonstrate, backed by suitable material, the enjoyment which the children can gain from reading works of fiction.

One method is to liken fiction to the pupils own essays. This can be reinforced by checking with the English teacher beforehand what topics the pupils may have been writing about in the same week as the library session. The librarian can then select books with passages on the same topic e.g. holidays, show the books to the class and read passages from the books.

Another distinguishing feature of fiction is that events in the books can also happen to the pupils in their own lives. Children's fiction is now rich in realistic stories of ordinary children coping with family situations. If the librarian can persuade the pupils to ally themselves with characters in books then the pupils may realize that fiction in the library deals with events which are not alien to their own lives inside and outside school.

Having discussed fiction with the class, the librarian can then either let the pupils browse among the shelves or take groups around the fiction shelves, asking what the pupils' preferences are and pointing out suitable novels which would interest individual pupils. The class should be allowed time to look at books and make a reasonable choice, if a choice is made. The practice of giving pupils two minutes to choose a book and return to their place is counterproductive as the pupils will feel pressurized into choosing a book, *any* book, merely to obey the wishes of the teacher or librarian. If the children are better informed of the choice of books and are actively aided in their choice, they will choose books in a positive manner and will be less likely to choose a book which does not interest them and which they will not read. Forcing children to read a library book, of any kind, will give them a totally imbalanced view of the purpose of the school library.

In explaining the concept of non-fiction, the librarian should follow a similar pattern as with fiction. It is again important to stress that non-fiction, both books and non-book materials, are already a part of the pupils' home and school life. In history, geography, science, maths etc. the textbooks used are all non-fiction. They are books of fact. A short explanation of non-fiction might be that it includes material, of a quickfactual nature, on everything under the sun as well as the sun itself.

The librarian can ask for examples of non-fiction books or media used in the home or in school. Examples such as recipe books, football yearbooks, telephone directories, maps etc. can be used to identify the material in the library with the pupils' lives outside school. As with fiction, the librarian must have a plentiful supply of non-fiction material which can be shown to the class and which the class can examine individually.

At this point it will be useful for the librarian to explain to the pupils the idea that non-fiction material deals with different *subjects*. This will plant an idea in the minds of the class and the idea will be developed later. The librarian can show the infinite variety of subjects in non-fiction by choosing a cross section of material from different areas.

Another aspect of non-fiction material is the difference in lay-out between fiction and non-fiction books. The librarian can point out the parts of a non-fiction book which make it immediately identifiable i.e. the contents page, illustrations, maps and most important, *the index*.

The librarian will have to decide whether it is better to explain the parts of a book, especially the index, before teaching the skills of catalogue use and the concept of classification. The index is the most vital aspect of non-fiction material and while this should be stressed, it is not very useful to laboriously explain to pupils all the parts of a book and how a book is made. The pupils have no *need* for this information. A compromise may be struck by briefly teaching the workings of the index but leaving the main explanation until later, when dealing with encyclopaedias and reference books in general.

Finally, the librarian should attempt to show that the main use of non-fiction material in the library will be for information. Once the pupils can see non-fiction in this light, they will be more able to select the information they need by using the index. Examples can be given of selecting information for project work or homework. The librarian can use examples in conjunction with one of the pupils' teachers so that the examples will be of immediate relevance. If the class has been studying animals in science, the librarian can show the pupils how to use an index to select certain facts which they require e.g. when are the young of certain species born?

An analogy which will be used throughout the following chapters, is that of the telephone directory. The librarian can refer to this many times, showing pupils that when they use non-fiction material and select information by means of an index, the process is similar to that of using a telephone directory. Only the information gained is different. The idea of gaining information from a library may be an unfamiliar concept for the pupils and the librarian will repeat this idea, using the telephone analogy, many times before it is accepted.

In teaching the concepts of fiction and non-fiction and the difference between the two, the librarian is introducing other ideas for library use, which will be repeated later. The class will also have been given the opportunity to browse around the shelves, identifying the different material. By introducing a variety of skills at this stage, the librarian will be avoiding the trap of merely stating what fiction and non-fiction mean and then setting the children a test to gauge their understanding of the concepts. The teaching of the concepts fiction and non-fiction should not be an end in itself but a means towards introducing to pupils the idea of the library system as something which is easily used and understood and the school library as an integral part of the school, useful for both education and recreational pursuits.

EXAMPLES.

The pupils will appreciate the idea of fiction and non-fiction if they can have first hand experience of the material. The librarian can, before the class comes to the library, arrange groups of books and non-book materials which include fiction and non-fiction material. When the class comes to the library, it can be separated into groups, each with one pile of books. A game can be devized where the group has to sort out the fiction from the non-fiction; link together fiction and non-fiction material on a similar topic; arrange the fiction by author and the non-fiction by class number. The materials to be used might include (fiction first):

(a). WILLIAMSON, H.: Tarka the otter. Bodley Head, 1965.
WHITLOCK, R.: Otters. Priory Press, 1974.
(b). STRONG, L.A.G.: The fifth of November. H. Hamilton, 1965.
WINSTOCK, L.: Gunpowder, treason and plot. Wayland, 1973.
(c). TREECE, H.: Horned helmet. Penguin, 1965.
ROBERTS, M.: Fury of the Vikings. Chambers, 1977.
(d). WELCH, R.: Knight crusader. O.U.P., 1954.
BAILEY, V. *and*
WISE, E.: The crusades. Longman, 1969.
(e). WALTERS, H.: Spaceship to Saturn. Faber and Faber, 1967.
SILCOCK, B.: Pathways in space. Dent, 1964.

(f). DARKE, M.: A question of courage. Penguin, 1975.
      JACKDAW No. 49: Women in revolt. Jackdaw, 1968.
(g). HARDCASTLE, M.: Soccer is also a game. Heinemann, 1966.
      BEBBINGTON, J.: Soccer sidelines. Evans Bros., 1974.

Chapter Six

The Promotion of Fiction

For some teachers and librarians, the advent of teaching methods which make more use of libraries in schools has been accompanied by a decline in the traditional use of the school library, i.e. the reading of fiction. Too much emphasis, such people would argue, has been placed on inquiry skills dealing with non-fiction material in the school library at the expense of the 'true' library material, the fiction. This argument, however, implies that teaching the use of non-fiction material is in some way deleterious to teaching the use of fiction. This is not the case. Both fiction and non-fiction should be exploited and not separately, but together. Many children will become interested in non-fiction books by reading a fiction book. For instance, if a pupil reads Rosemary Sutcliff's 'Eagle of the ninth' the same pupil may turn to non-fiction books, such as 'Roman Britain' by Philip Sauvain, or non-book materials, such as 'The Roman occupation, 2: weapons' a Gateway filmstrip, which deal with the Roman Empire, Roman Britain or Roman uniforms and weapons. So any attempt to teach library skills must include the active promotion of fiction within the library.

How does the librarian do this? Firstly it must be said that the librarian cannot, in isolation, create a continuing interest in fiction amongst pupils in a school. There must be close contact with the English department (but not only the English department, as other teachers in the school will read children's fiction and can be equally helpful) concerning the selection of books and the suitability of different books for different pupils. (See chapter 4.)

Given this contact with the teachers, the librarian can, in the library, stimulate interest in fiction by actually taking the fiction to the pupils, showing them books, reading parts of books, asking them about books, displaying books, playing cassette recordings of fiction, linking fiction books with non-fiction materials, having the pupils talk about, draw scenes from books and perhaps even act out scenes from books they have read.

The promotion of fiction in the school library must be done well if it is to attract the attention of the pupils. At home, the pupils will be bombarded by television, radio and newspaper advertisements, trying to convince them that they should buy a certain record, eat a certain chocolate bar but not that they should read a certain book. It is against such standards that the librarian must compete. Placing books on the shelves or on display, therefore, will only attract the attention of the keen readers, who will read anyway. The librarian will be hoping to show the non-readers or reluctant readers (who may be reluctant because of the choice of books they are offered) the enjoyment which can be obtained from fiction. Librarians should not be afraid to argue that fiction-reading can be an end in itself, a purely pleasurable experience. The prime method of presenting fiction is for the librarian him/herself to read the book, then take it to the pupils and talk to them about it.

If we take Robert Westall's excellent book 'The machine-gunners' as an example, we can follow how the librarian can interest the pupils in . this book and other books on a similar topic. 'The machine-gunners' is an exciting tale of the discovery of a crashed German aeroplane by Chas, who is looking for souvenirs after an air raid during the Second World War. Chas and his friends manage to extract the machine-gun and its ammunition from the aeroplane and hide it from their parents, school-teachers and the local policeman. Hoping to use the gun to repel German invaders, the boys almost cause a disaster when they take a group of Polish soldiers to be Germans. What distinguishes 'The machine-gunners' from other children's books is that it captures, very precisely, the ideas, feelings and words of the boys. The boys jealously collect war souvenirs, they fight, they swear, they listen to their parents' conversations while remaining apparently invisible and they dream of fighting the Germans. The book is sympathetic to all its characters, adults, children and the German rear-gunner captured by the boys.

What the librarian can do with the book is firstly show it to the pupils. The cover, which is brightly coloured and looks attractive, shows a scene from the book in which the boys transport the machine-gun in a bogie to their hideout.

This book has an interesting cover which will draw the pupils' attention. The librarian can then capitalize on this interest by briefly outlining the plot, without giving away too much of the story. Perhaps more importantly, the librarian can discuss the qualities of the book which the pupils will find attractive: the humour of the book, the excitement and suspense, the struggle between adults and children and the feeling of how ordinary people lived during the war and adjusted to it.

To do this successfully, the librarian should always read part of the book to the pupils. In 'The machine-gunners' a passage which would appeal to the pupils, giving them a taste of the book's humour as well as showing them the attitude of the children to each other and to authority in the shape of parents, teachers, policeman, is the list of rules or 'Standing Orders' for the children's 'fortress'. A passage such as this is worthwhile reading aloud because it will immediately capture the children's interest and imagination. It will also help to demonstrate to the pupils that the book will appeal to them because of its content and not only because the librarian has recommended it.

'. . . a notice board marked *Fortress Caparetto — Standing Orders*. Chas was not quite sure what Standing Orders were, so they were read out twice a day, with everybody standing up respectfully.

1. Anyone who steals food from the Fortress, if found guilty by Court Martial, shall be thrown into the goldfish pond. They may take off any clothes they want to first, but Keep It Decent.
2. Anyone touching the Gun without permission will be chucked out of the Fortress for Three Months. Anyone who speaks to Bodser Brown for any reason will be chucked out for good.
3. Anyone lying on the banks will tidy up afterwards.
4. No peeing within fifty yards, or Anything Else.
5. Always come in by the back fence, after making sure you're not followed.
6. No stealing from shops without permission. All goods stolen belong to the Fortress.
7. Only sentries will touch the air-rifle. Hand back all pellets out of your pockets etc. when coming off duty.
8. Do.not mess about with catapults inside the Fortress or you will wash up for four days.
9. Do not mess about at all.
10. Penalty for splitting to parents, teachers etc. is DEATH.
11. Do not waste anything.
12. Anybody who brings in useless old junk will take it back to the Tip where they got it.
13. Quartermaster gives out all the eats. Don't argue with her.[1]

Having shown the book to the pupils and having read part of it, the librarian will have interested a number, if not all, of the pupils in the book. The problem which then faces the librarian, is that there may only be one copy of 'The machine-gunners' in the library and only one pupil can read it at any time. There is a danger that the librarian, in creating a demand for the book which cannot be satisfied immediately, will cause friction in the class because only one pupil can have the book. There is also the danger that by showing the book to be of great interest and quality, the librarian may be presenting an image of the book as something which is precious and to be sought after to the exception of all other books. Thus when the librarian is encouraging pupils to read novels, there should always be a number of books which can be shown or read to the pupils. The librarian can choose a topic (in this case the Second World War) and present a few books which might interest the pupils and lead them from one book to another.

The need to show a number of books will also be important if the librarian is to take into account the different reading abilities of the pupils in a class. Also, the librarian should not present books which will appeal only to boys or to girls but should pick a topic which can interest both sexes. If we take the Second World War as our (broad) topic, we can see how it is possible to bring fiction to the pupils and awaken their interest in books of this kind.

Following on from 'The machine-gunners' which would appeal to all pupils, the librarian might then choose another book of wide interest, 'The silver sword' by Ian Serrailler, a story about a family which is separated when the father and mother are taken away by the Germans. The children then have to survive on their own, despite the privations of war-time existence. Joined by another boy, Jan, the children set out to find their parents and the hazardous journey takes them from Poland to Switzerland. 'The silver sword' is a very moving story, but told in a straightforward, unsentimental way. Like 'The machine-gunners', 'The silver sword' would appeal to both boys and girls, but it is a different type of book. This might be illustrated by reading a passage which is in contrast to that read from 'The machine-gunners'. In this passage, Edek, one of the three children, tries to stop the Germans taking his mother away.

'In the ceiling was a small trapdoor that led into the attic. A ladder lay between his bed and the wall. Quietly he removed it, locked it under the trap and climbed up. Hidden between the water tank and the felt jacket round it was his rifle . . . Looking out of the window into the street, he saw a Nazi van waiting outside the front door. Two storm troopers were taking his mother down the steps and she was struggling.

Quietly Edek lifted the window sash till it was half open. He dared not shoot in case he hit his mother . . .

His first shot hit a soldier in the arm . . . With the next two shots Edek aimed at the tyres. One punctured the car wheel, but the van got away . . . (he) ran down to his sisters . . . Bronia was sitting up in bed and Ruth was trying to calm her. She was almost as distraught herself. Only the effort to comfort Bronia kept her from losing control'.[2]

Another book dealing with war-time experiences, is 'A kind of secret weapon' by Elliott Arnold, which tells of a boy, Peter, whose parents produce an anti-German underground newspaper in war-time Denmark. It is a well-written, very gripping book and pupils would be attracted by the way the reader, in certain incidents, is kept in suspense. One such incident, worth reading aloud, concerns a risky trip which Peter has to make to deliver a packet of papers to a woman in a newspaper kiosk in Copenhagen.

'He was almost there and now he was there and he walked past the kiosk not only because he just couldn't bring himself to walk up to it but because out of the corner of his eye he saw someone inside the kiosk — and it was not a tall, thin woman . . .

Peter did not know exactly what to do. He guessed there was an exact time that the packet should be delivered . . . In any case, he could not stand there on the street corner, looking like a country bumpkin, looking even more like a lost schoolboy, attracting attention, attracting questions . . .

As he approached the kiosk again, he felt a tinge of excitement. But this time his heart was not pounding as it had before and he did not know whether it was just that he was cold and wanted to get rid of the packet and go home.

As he came to the kiosk, he saw there was a tall, thin woman behind the counter this time . . .'.[3]

'A kind of secret weapon' is an adventure story, full of incident which could be read by most pupils of average ability. When choosing books on a particular topic, the librarian will choose books suitable for the class, but within that class there may be a wide range of reading abilities. Thus for certain pupils, the librarian will have to choose books which are, on the one hand, not too easy for above-average pupils, and, on the other hand, not too difficult for less able pupils.

Two examples which illustrate this point, on the topic of the Second World War might be, for more able pupils, 'Thunder and lightnings' by Jan Mark and for slower readers, 'Anne Frank' retold by John Kennett.

'Thunder and lightnings' is a book which deals with the relationship of two boys, from different social backgrounds. One of the boys, Victor, has a fascination for Lightning aircraft, which were used in World War II but (in the story) face the possibility of being replaced by more modern planes. It is a very sensitive book which would be enjoyed by able readers but which might prove difficult for some average pupils and for less able pupils.

'Anne Frank' is a book designed to be read by slower readers. It is based on 'The diary of Anne Frank' and quotes passages from the original book, whilst relating the story in a series of short chapters. It is simply written but keeps the narrative qualities of the original, the suspense, the horror, the romance, so that the pupils can appreciate the tale without being overwhelmed by the language.

Other books which could be shown to pupils (and read to them) on the same topic, include 'When Hitler stole pink rabbit' by Judith Kerr, the story of a nine year old girl whose family has to flee from Germany in 1933; 'The great escape' by Paul Brickhill, which tells of an attempted breakout from a prison camp; 'Colditz story' by P.R. Reid, also deals with prison camp escapes; 'We couldn't leave Dinah' by Mary Treadgold, an exciting book which combines the story of a Channel Island taken over by the Germans and that of a pony called Dinah; 'They didn't come back' by Paul Berna, in which an unexplained tragedy of the Second World War is explored by some children who come to live in a new town; 'Backwater war' by Peggy Woodford, whose main character is a girl growing up in the Channel Islands which are occupied by the Germans.[4]

Having collected a group of books on a topic of interest, the librarian can show the pupils a variety of novels ranging from the simply written to the more advanced type of fiction. With this range, the librarian, with the teacher's assistance, can approach the promotion of fiction on a class level, but also, and perhaps more importantly, on an individual level. The ideal library situation, which may never be always achieved but should always be aimed for, is that each pupil will be helped (if help is needed) in the selection of a novel, which is suitable to his/her interests, age and reading ability. By presenting a group of books, such as those mentioned above, the librarian can go some way towards this ideal.

Once the librarian has shown the books to the pupils, it is important that, once the books are taken out by the pupils, the librarian finds out the response to certain books. The books offered will only become popular if the pupils read them, enjoy them and communicate this enjoyment to their friends. The pupil's response can be gauged in different ways, by pupils talking about a book they have read, by writing about it or perhaps by drawing a scene from it.

The librarian and teacher can gain much inside knowledge about the books they have recommended and selected, by listening to what the pupils have to say about certain books. There are dangers. Some pupils will be able to articulate their enjoyment more freely than others. Thus whereas one boy, who has the confidence to speak in front of the class, may explain in detail why he felt that he could share in the excitement of Peter, the boy in 'A kind of secret weapon', another boy, less extrovert, may be intimidated by having to talk to the class. If the latter feels that he *has* to talk about each book he reads, he may well be put off reading books. On the other hand, the same boy may well explain to the librarian, in private, that while he thought 'A kind of secret weapon' was a gripping book, he also thought that too much happened to Peter in the book, which made it less appealing. It is better in this case, for the librarian to articulate this boy's feelings to the class and leave the boy free to read and enjoy more novels without the fear of having to stand up and talk in class.

Some pupils will enjoy writing about characters in a novel they have read, but as with talking about books, certain pupils will be more able to write about books than others. A girl who is a slow reader, may read and enjoy 'Anne Frank' but may have great difficulty in expressing her feelings about the book in her own words. Thus while it may help the girl to write an account of a scene in a book, the fact that she reads 'Anne Frank' should not automatically mean that she has to produce a piece of written work. The librarian is trying to encourage the reading of novels in the school, especially among pupils who are unlikely to read without encouragement, so if there are fewer potential barriers to reading, there will be a greater likelihood of less able pupils coming to the library and asking for books.

One method used to encourage pupils to write about incidents in novels is for the librarian or teacher to provide extracts from novels for those pupils who may not have read complete books. The pupils can then write about the extract or be asked to imagine what might happen next in the novel. For example, what does the pupil think will happen to Edek, in 'The silver sword'? Will the soldiers return to capture him? What will happen to his sisters? This, of course, is another way of enticing pupils to read the book.

Many pupils will write excellent criticisms of books they have read. One way of showing the pupils' attitudes to other pupils is for the librarian to pin book reviews or reports on the library walls or notice boards. Thus if one pupil writes ecstatically about 'The gunners' the librarian may pin the review on the wall and write underneath 'Do you agree with Paul?' It is also likely that the librarian will receive conflicting critiques of a particular book and there may be even more response if two pupils read 'Thunder and lightnings' but disagreed over its worth. The librarian can then pose the question 'Do you agree with Kerrie or with Stephen?'.

Another method of publicising books in the school library is for the librarian to ask pupils to draw a picture in connection with a book they have read. The picture could be a new cover for 'The machine-gunners' or a drawing of one of the aeroplanes in 'Thunder and lightnings' or a sketch of Dinah, the horse in 'We couldn't leave Dinah'. Again these could be put up in the library or could be the basis of a library competition. The librarian could also suggest to the art teacher that fiction might be a theme for some of the pupils' work in school.[5]

Similarly, if the pupils have a drama course in school, they could act out a scene or scenes from a book some or all of them have read. Some of the chapters from 'A silver sword' would be ideal for such a project.[6]

Each school will have different methods and ideas on the promotion of fiction but if the pupils are to read novels and enjoy them, there must be enthusiasm on the part of the librarian and the teacher, plus a willingness to let the pupils decide for themselves whether or not they like a book once they have read it. If the librarian and teacher can accept that some pupils will not respond to certain books recommended by them and by other pupils, then they will be able to discover, by reading and recommending books other books, what the pupils *do* enjoy. Above all, fiction in the school library should be experienced by the pupils themselves, with suggestions from the librarian, but without any feeling on the part of the pupils that they are being forced to read books against their will.

1. 'The machine gunners' Pages 88—89.
2. 'The silver sword' Pages 33—34.

3. 'A kind of secret weapon' Pages 66—67.
4. Books and non-book materials listed in this chapter:-
   ARNOLD, E.: A kind of secret weapon. Longman, 1969.
   BERNA, P.: They didn't come back. Bodley Head, 1969.
   BRICKHILL, P.: The great escape. Faber, 1946.
   GATEWAY: The Roman occupation 2: weapons (filmstrip). Gateway 197—.
   KENNETT, J.: Anne Frank: a story based on her diary. Blackie, 1974.
   KERR, J.: When Hitler stole pink rabbit. Collins, 1971.
   MARK, J.: Thunder and lightnings, Penguin Books, 1976.
   REID, R.R.: Colditz story. Hodder and Stoughton, 1962.
   SAUVAIN, P.: Roman Britain. Macmillan 1976.
   SERRAILLER, I.: The silver sword. Penguin Books, 1969.
   SUTCLIFF, R.: The eagle of the ninth. O.U.P. 1954.
   TREADGOLD, M.: We couldn't leave Dinah. Cape, 1965.
   WESTALL, R.: The machine gunners, Macmillan, 1975.
   WOODFORD, P.: Backwater war. Bodley Head, 1975.
5. For the display of fiction in the school library, see chapter 11.
6. A comprehensive list of ways of encouraging pupils to respond to fiction is given in 'Children's literature in education' volume 8 No. 3, Autumn 1977. 'Twenty-four things to do with a book' by Geoff Fox.

Chapter Seven

Classification

The concept of classification puzzles many library users, both adults and children. It is often seen as a fiendish plot by librarians to confuse and confound readers. This is usually the case because of a lack of education of the readers by the librarian. In a school library, the librarian will be seeking to prove to the pupils that the library is a part of each subject they study as well as a recreational source. If the pupils are taught how to use the library effectively, they will appreciate its usefulness. They cannot, however, appreciate the library without understanding why it is arranged in what appears to be a strange manner.

The librarian's task is to show that library classification is a numerical extension of the classification which exists in every part of the children's lives. The pupils can be shown how, without classification in society, without the grouping of people and things in a logical order, chaos would result. Thus people are classified into men, women, boys, girls, children, adults etc. and without these distinctions in classes or groups being made, society would break down. Classification exists at every point in life. Any description of a person, for example, involves classification. The librarian can describe him/herself to the children as an example of classification. Thus the librarian is male/female; dark-haired/fair haired etc.; brown-eyed/blue-eyed etc.; thin/fat etc.; married/single; Scottish/English etc. All descriptions place people into groups or classes, so the librarian is identified as part of a group i.e. librarians, just as the gym teacher is recognized as part of a group i.e. gym teachers.

The prime examples are the pupils themselves. Schools, being highly structured at all levels, are excellent examples of classification. The librarian can show the pupils that they are divided into groups within the school and that this is reflected in the names of their forms. For example, if the class being taught is $2N_2$, the librarian can use this notation, used by the children each day as an instance of classification. The pupils can be asked what the '2' denotes — second year. Then what the 'N' means — Napier House. Then what the '2' means — the second group within the second year of Napier House. Already the children are showing the librarian that they can understand quite complex examples of classification.

It can then be explained to the pupils that the above example of classification follows the general rule in libraries i.e. that subjects are firstly classified into large groups — as with second year; then into smaller groups — second year, Napier House; then even smaller groups groups — second year, Napier House, second group or class. On the library shelves the pupils will find that all books on animals will be placed near each other but, as with school classes, they are arranged in a predetermined fashion, from general to specific. All books on animals as a whole (as with second year) will be at the beginning, followed by books on smaller groups of animals, birds for instance (as with second year, Napier House). Within the books on birds, there will be books on groups of specific birds, owls for example (as with second year, Napier House, second class).

There is no need to mention, at this point, the numerical aspects of shelf classification. The librarian will be dealing with Dewey Decimal System (or any other system used in the library) at a later stage and to introduce numbers at this stage would confuse the pupils. It is the *idea* of classification that the librarian must firstly explain.

A practical example of how library classification reflects that used outside school is the analogy, used by many librarians, of the supermarket. Almost all pupils will have used a supermarket and the librarian, by asking the pupils about the arrangement of the stock in the supermarket, can provide the pupils with an excellent example of (nonnumerical) shelf classification.

The pupils will have noticed that in a supermarket, groups or classes of articles, are shelved together. Why, the librarian can ask, are all the articles, tins, packets, vegetables, household goods etc. not placed on the shelves in any order? The pupils will know the answer, that the shelf arrangement facilitates ease of access and discovery. This, the librarian can explain, is identical to library shelf classification where all books and non-book materials on one subject (group, class) are shelved together, for ease of access and discovery.

Thus if a person in a supermarket wants a tin of soup, he will find it in the food section (large class); then the tinned food section (small class); then the tinned soup section (smaller class). In the school library if a girl is looking for material on birds, she will find it in the non-fiction section (large class); then the animals section (smaller class); then the birds section (smaller class).

In this way, the librarian can make the pupils explain why the library classification exists and how it is similar to classification in a supermarket. A more specific point can be made by comparing the search for a particular article, a tin of *tomato* soup, in a supermarket and a particular item, a book or filmstrip on owls, in the school library. The particular 'class' of soup to be found i.e. *tomato*, will form yet another smaller class within the larger class of tinned soups. In the supermarket, the tins of soup will not be mixed up but separated into groups (or classes) such as tomato, lentil etc. So in the library, the particular 'class' of bird to be found i.e. *owl*, will form yet another smaller class within the larger class, birds. All books or films or cassettes on owls will be shelved together, as will books on vultures, eagles etc.

Having explained why the classification scheme is necessary and how it is arranged, the librarian has then to demonstrate, in practical terms, classification aids to the retrieval of the desired material. Returning to the supermarket analogy, the pupils may be asked how they find the different sections (classes) in the supermarket. The reply will be two-fold. One the one hand a person in a supermarket can walk around *all* the shelves and eventually find the desired material i.e. a tin of tomato soup. On the other hand that person can follow the signs in the super-market, where there may be large signs such as FOOD and within that section (class), smaller signs such as SOUP or BREAD. Thus there exist in supermarkets, some classification aids which facilitate the retrieval of material.

The librarian can now proceed to explain what is perhaps the most puzzling aspect of libraries to adults and children alike, the numerical system.[1] The idea of supermarket guides is a useful introduction be-cause the pupils will be able to understand that guides are also needed in the school library. The librarian must now explain why a more com-plicated system of guidance is needed in libraries than in supermarkets.

The most obvious difference in a library, the librarian can point out, is that while a shopper will recognize a tin of tomato soup by its shape, colour and its label (which faces outwards from the shelf), a reader in a library cannot use the same criteria for a book or filmstrip on owls, because all books and filmstrips look similar when on the shelves and their 'labels' may not face outwards from the shelf or may not be easy to read. Some guide is necessary to the contents of the book or filmstrip and the system used in most libraries is the numerical system.

In the case of the numerical system, the librarian can demonstrate that such a system is not alien to the pupils' own experiences. Where else do they encounter a numerical system? In school, the librarian might ask, how do you find Mr McEwan's room? Go to 2.24, the answer might be. How do you find that? The answer will be: go to the second floor and to room 24 on that floor.

The pupils have, from their answers, shown two things to the librarian. Firstly, that in school a numerical system exists which they understand. Secondly, that the numerals are a notation to a classification scheme. The '2' represents a particular floor in the class 'floors' and the '24' represents a particular room i.e. Mr McEwan's, in the class 'rooms'. The class 'rooms' forms a smaller class within the larger class 'floors'.

Another analogy, representing a simple numerical system, which the librarian can use is that of the cutlery drawer. The librarian can ask the pupils to imagine that, at home, the cutlery drawer was marked 1, 2 and 3 in a 3-sectional tray. Beside the tray there would be a guide indicating that knives went in section 1, forks in section 2 and spoons in section 3. With this method, a person who was replacing spoons would know, without looking inside the tray, that the spoons went in section 3. This would represent a classification system which the pupils will recognize and a numerical guide to that system.

The above examples of simple numerical systems will be easily understood by the pupils. The librarian has then to explain that because a library deals with an infinite number of subjects, groups or classes, a more complex numerical system is required.

Few children will have heard of the Dewey Decimal Classification and while it is worthwhile for the librarian to tell the pupils the name of the inventor of the system, a detailed explanation of the scheme is not necessary. Whether the pupils remember the name of the classification scheme is of no consequence. It will not help them to retrieve information in the school library. Briefly, the librarian can show (perhaps by using an overhead projector) the outline of the scheme, which uses the numbers 001—999. There is no point in asking the pupils to try to remember the numbers of the main classes or to have the pupils copy down parts of the scheme. This will be confusing and fruitless.

The pupils can be shown that each number represents a subject or a class. The librarian should have a number of books and non-book materials on hand to demonstrate this point. Thus an item on sport in general, will have the number 796 and all books on the general aspect of sport will be shelved at this number. Pupils should not be asked to remember the class number (the term 'call number' is also used) of every book or cassette they take from the shelves but the librarian can suggest that the pupils treat the class numbers on library books and media as they would telephone numbers. That is, to remember only those numbers used most frequently.

Many adults who use libraries are confused by the use of decimals in classification numbers. In a school library, this may be less of a problem where pupils are accustomed to using decimals in schools. The librarian must show how and why decimals are used in the classification scheme. Having already shown the use of numerals (and decimals) in the guide to school rooms, the librarian can explain that, because the library has material on thousands of different subjects, a simple notation similar to that used with school rooms is not sufficient. Also, decimals allow subjects to be expressed more specifically and the librarian can return to the analogy of telephone numbers to explain this point.

In a small town where only a few hundred people own a telephone, the numbers can be simple, as in, for example, Littletown 329. In larger towns and in cities, more complex numbers are needed. Thus a London number might be 01–667–1215.

Pupils in schools are familiar with telephone numbers and they can remember numbers of 7 or 8 digits. The librarian can ask the children which telephone numbers they remember and why they remember those numbers and not others. The pupils will explain that they associate a telephone number with a specific person, a relative or friend. In the library, it can be shown that they will be able to associate a number with a specific subject and, with constant use, they will remember the number.

It is worthwhile for the librarian to show, perhaps with an overhead projector, how numbers in the library are built up and how they are similar to telephone numbers. Thus the number for material in the library on North West England is 914.27. This number is derived from the building up from a general number 900 to the specific number 914.27 and may be shown as follows:

900	History and geography.
910	General geography.

914	Geography of Europe.
914.2	Geography of Great Britain.
914.27	Geography of North West England.

Similarly the telephone number in London can be broken down into

01-	London.
01-667-	Specific area of London.
01-667-1215	Specific telephone in that area of London.

The librarian will use a local telephone number to illustrate this point.

The building of numbers can also be shown by using books from the shelves and the librarian can show how the subject of each subsequent book becomes more specific.

Teaching classification and the use of the Dewey Decimal Classification must be done carefully and slowly. It cannot all be done in one lesson, because of the complexity of the concepts being introduced and the intricacies of the numerical system. Most of the points will need to be repeated, in different forms, using different examples from books and non-book materials in the school library.

As some classes and some pupils will respond more quickly or more slowly to the ideas being taught, the librarian must adequately prepare for each period of teaching classification skills, adapting each lesson to the needs and capabilities of individual groups of pupils and individual pupils within these groups. Because the pupils' future use and appreciation of the school library will be, to some extent, shaped by their understanding of how and why the library is arranged in a definite order, the librarian must devote sufficient time for the preparation of the lessons, so that the pupils will be able to fully assimilate the ideas being explained by the librarian.

1. It is being assumed that the school library will be classified by the Dewey Decimal Classification system. Librarians using other systems could however, use the suggestions and analogies which follow in explaining their own classification schemes.

Chapter Eight

The Catalogue

The catalogue[1] in the school library is the heart of the library system. It can be seen as something into which information is fed and from which information is pumped out to every section of the library. The catalogue contains, in a compact form, proof of the existence of all the material held by the library, whether that material be on the library shelves, located in another department in the school, or on loan to staff or pupil. By using the catalogue and *appreciating* its use, pupils will find the library less complicated and material more easily retrieved.

In a recent article[2] Michael Marland wrote '. . . the indexing systems made available in libraries are not used by the children.' The reason for this may be that children either do not know how to use the catalogue in the school library or they may not have been convinced of the increase in the efficiency of retrieval which follows the use of the catalogue. The librarian's task is, therefore, twofold. Firstly the pupils must be taught the mechanics of the catalogue i.e. how it works and secondly, they must be made aware of the beneficial effects which follow its proper use.

Before teaching the skills needed to make greatest use of the catalogue, the librarian must study the approach to the teaching of these skills. A librarian can teach classification skills to a fairly large group of pupils and succeed in fully explaining the concepts in hand. When teaching skills involving catalogue use, the librarian must realize that what is needed is a *practical* demonstration of how to use the catalogue in order to retrieve information from the material in the library. Secondly, the explanation of catalogue use should be done at the catalogue itself. If the librarian uses only a slide/tape sequence or a series of slides or overhead projections (all useful up to a point) he/she will find that the pupils, when confronted with using the catalogue, may not be able to remember the steps involved. Thirdly, the teaching must be done in small groups, so that each group can be gathered around the catalogue and follow the librarian's practical explanation. If larger groups are used, some pupils may not be able to see the librarian point out, for example, the class number on a catalogue card.

The first part of the catalogue to be described by the librarian is the author catalogue, which will list both fiction and non-fiction books and also non-book materials (possibly under the title). If a pupil is looking for a fiction book, the author catalogue may well be superfluous and it must be stressed that if a pupil knows the author and title of a book which is in the school library, the pupil will *not* need to look in the catalogue. The author catalogue will be used to find out (a) if the library has any books by a certain author and (b) which books by that author the library holds. In practical terms, with regard to fiction, the author catalogue may often be more useful to the librarian than to the pupils. When explaining the use of the author catalogue for fiction, the librarian should always complete the retrieval process i.e. the pupils should be shown how to look up a certain author and title and how to go to the shelves and find the book. The librarian will make sure that the example being used is actually on the shelves before the teaching of catalogue use.

For use with non-fiction books and non-book materials the author catalogue will also be necessary. With this function to be explained, the librarian can return to the analogy of the telephone. When a pupil wishes to telephone a person whose number is unknown, the pupil will consult the telephone directory to find out the person's telephone number. So in the school library, if a pupil wishes to find a non-fiction book by a certain author (provided by the class teacher perhaps), the author catalogue will provide the pupil with the author's name and the number at which the book is classified.

In a telephone directory, there may be several people with the same names and initials, e.g. J. BROWN. The pupil looking for the particular J. Brown distinguishes that person by his address. In the library an author J. BROWN may have written several books and the pupil will only find the number of the book by distinguishing the particular title which is recommended.

Once again the librarian must complete the process by selecting a given author and title, looking it up in the author catalogue, then taking the pupils to the shelves and finding the book. If the librarian merely

shows the pupils how to find the number of the book, but does not explain how the book is found, the pupils may well be puzzled. This is the
equivalent of showing a child how to find someone's telephone number,
but failing to show the child how the telephone works, so that the child
can actually speak to the desired person.

Librarians may choose, to avoid confusion, only to show the system
being successfully operated, but pupils should be told, if not shown, that
usage of the author catalogue does not ensure success. If, for example,
a pupil looks up a filmstrip under its title, finds the class number,
goes to the shelves but does not find the material which is sought, the
pupil must be aware that another reader may have borrowed that filmstrip and that it will have to be reserved. It might be useful, therefore,
for the librarian to demonstrate an unsuccessful search for a book and
explain the library's reservation system.

The subject index and classified catalogue should not be explained
separately but should be seen as two parts of one process. The subject
index is akin to the headings in the 'Yellow Pages' of a telephone book
and the classified catalogue is akin to the lists of names, addresses and
telephone numbers under the headings in the 'Yellow Pages'. The librarian, as a prelude to teaching catalogue use, may show the pupils how a
'Yellow Pages' works, by looking up a 'subject' or 'class' or category of
services. An example might be hospitals. The pupils will be shown how
'hospitals' is found by following the 'subject' headings in alphabetical
order and finding, under hospitals, a list of names and addresses with
telephone numbers.

So in the catalogue, the pupils can be shown, a subject — hospitals
for instance — will be found by looking in the subject index, in alphabetical order for the heading 'hospitals'. In the subject index, there will
be a number (or numbers) for hospitals. The subject index cards might
read

HOSPITALS: MEDICAL TREATMENT 610
HOSPITALS: SOCIAL SERVICES   362.3

In the classified catalogue, under the numbers 610 and 362.3, there will
be a series of cards, denoting the material held by the library on this
topic. This is exactly the same as the list of hospitals in the 'Yellow
Pages'. The librarian can also repeat what has been said before, that in
order to get through to a hospital, the pupil will have to find the number
and dial it i.e. use the number to some purpose. So with a book or a

set of slides on hospitals, the pupil will have to find the number (by looking up the subject index) and use it (by looking up the classified catalogue or by going straight to the shelves).

The pupils therefore have two choices when they find the number (or numbers) they require. The librarian must explain what is sometimes a difficult concept for children to grasp. That is, that when a pupil is looking for some information, but not a lot of information, on a topic or when the pupil is looking for a book, any book, on a topic of non-curricular interest (a hobby perhaps), then the pupil may consult the subject index, find the number(s) and go directly to the shelves to find out what is available at that particular time.

It is when a pupil is seeking detailed information on a topic — a project perhaps — that the pupil will have to consult the classified catalogue, so that he or she can find *all* the material which the library has on that subject (costume, motor cars, water, weather etc). This will enable the pupil to go to the shelves and find the material in the library *at that time*, but also to reserve any material which has been borrowed by other pupils. The librarian can again stress that using the catalogue whether for author or subject, does not guarantee success. Just as the telephone may be engaged when the pupil has phoned the number (i.e. successfully completed all but one of the steps in information retrieval) so the books or slides or cassettes the pupil is looking for may be out on loan.

The librarian may return to the hospital analogy to stress the point about the choice of use which the pupil may make of the number(s) found in the subject index. If the pupil looks in the 'Yellow Pages' under hospitals, he or she will find a list of different hospitals. In this list, the major hospitals, which deal with most *general* illnesses, are mentioned first. So if the pupil wanted *any* hospital, not a particular type (or class) of hospital, then the pupil could telelphone that hospital. This would be the same as finding the number(s) for hospitals in the subject index and going directly to the shelves.

If the pupil wanted a particular type of hospital, an eye clinic for example, the pupil would look down the list of hospitals, which deal with *specific* illnesses until he or she found the eye clinic. This would be the same as finding the number(s) for hospitals in the subject index and then consulting the classified catalogue to find the *specific* material the library held on the subject 'hospitals'.

Explaining to pupils how to use the subject index must be done, as has been said, at the catalogue. It will be useful if the librarian gathers the group around the catalogue and allows each pupil, in turn to choose a subject, look it up and go the shelves to find what material is available. This method also caters for pupils looking up subjects under different headings. The librarian can explain that the pupil should look up the specific subject he or she is looking for. If that subject heading does not appear in the subject index, then the pupil should look up a wider subject heading. For example, if a pupil is doing a botany project, he or she may be looking for information on a particular species of tree, the beech tree. If the pupil consults the subject index and finds no heading for 'beech tree' the librarian can stress that the pupil should not give up, but should look under the more general heading of 'trees'. Also, if the pupil has tried all headings he or she can think of, but is still unsuccessful, the pupil should be encouraged to always ask the librarian for help.

In a recent British Library report, it was stated that '. . . the catalogue is approached via its organization and the information contained in the different types of entry, rather than by adopting a problem centred approach.'[3] The implication of this statement is that teaching catalogue use is approached from the viewpoint of the librarian rather than the pupil. This is only partly true. The pupils will need to know the different parts of the catalogue before they can use the catalogue effectively. Thus the explanation of the parts of the catalogue will be an introduction to the catalogue, with examples of the problems pupils will face following this introduction.

The librarian's dilemma in this situation is how does the librarian show the pupils the difficulties faced when using the catalogue without picking out hypothetical examples which the pupils might not remember? An interesting answer to this problem may take the form of library games devised by the librarian. The object of the games should be, in this case, to familiarize the pupils with certain difficulties they might face in using the catalogue and to make the appreciation of these difficulties an enjoyable experience.

One of the major difficulties that all users of libraries face is alphabetical order. The different sequences in the catalogue of author, title and subject may appear confusing to the pupils. A few examples of alphabetical games might be:

1.   Splitting the class into three groups and having the groups arrange themselves by (a) surname (b) christian name (c) name of the street where pupils live. In each case the librarian will signal the start of the game when the pupils are sitting down and the first group to arrange

themselves correctly (and perhaps write down the alphabetical order) will be the winner.

2. Asking the pupils (or groups of pupils) to write down, in alphabetical order the names of twenty teachers in the school.

3. Giving each group of pupils a telephone directory and a YELLOW PAGES and asking them to look up the telephone numbers of 6 stated names and addresses. Then asking the pupils to suggest the names, addresses and telephone numbers of a bus station, railway station, plumber, health centre and hairdresser.

4. Asking each group to write down in alphabetical order the names of 6 birds, 6 fish, 6 members of the cat family, 6 breeds of dog etc.

In each of the above games, points can be given for 1st, 2nd, 3rd and 4th and at the end of the lesson, one group can be declared the winner. Games such as these will be more effective than asking pupils, as a class, to translate into alphabetical order examples written on a workcard or on the blackboard by the librarian. A postscript to the games could be the librarian demonstrating, with the aid of an overhead projector or with large made up catalogue cards (perhaps 18 inches square), how the pupils might be faced with an alphabetical sequence in the catalogue.

Another problem which will perplex pupils is find the subject they require in the SUBJECT INDEX. The difficulty which normally arises is that a pupil cannot exactly define the subject he/she is looking for and has trouble in finding a synonym for it. Allied to this is the problem of encouraging pupils to look up not just one subject in the index, but other, possibly related topics. Thus instead of merely looking up TOWNS, they might also look up CITIES, VILLAGES, LOCAL GOVERNMENT etc. A SYNONYMS game has to be devised. Such a game should be centred around the catalogue but should also involve encyclopaedias and reference works.

One such game would involve giving each group a broad topic (on which there is a variety of material in the school library) and having each group suggest possible headings to look up in the SUBJECT INDEX; numbers to be found on the shelves; a list of materials on the topic from the CLASSIFIED CATALOGUE); and a list of references given in the encyclopaedias. The librarian could also give each group a YELLOW PAGES to suggest possible names, addresses and telephone numbers connected with the group's topic.

For example, the topic OIL could be given to one group. (This would be especially relevant if the class had been studying fuels in science). In the SUBJECT INDEX (each group could have a specified time at the catalogue) the group might find the following headings:

OIL:	DRILLING	622
OIL:	ENGINES	621.43
OIL:	GEOLOGY	553
OIL:	PAINTING	751
OIL:	POLLUTION	574.5
OIL:	REFINING	665
OIL:	WELLS	622

In the YELLOW PAGES the group would find:

OIL BROKERS; OIL RUBBER MANUFACTURERS AND
SUPPLIERS; OIL BURNING APPLIANCES AND INSTAL-
LATION; OIL COMPANIES; OIL FIELD EQUIPMENT
MANUFACTURERS; OIL FUEL DISTRIBUTORS AND
SUPPLIERS. They would also find references to: HEATING
CONTRACTORS — DOMESTIC; PARAFFIN RETAILERS:
PETROLEUM PRODUCTS MANUFACTURERS.

In the OXFORD JUNIOR ENCYCLOPEDIA, the group would find, in the index:

OIL, mineral; OIL, natural; OILCAKE; OIL REFINING;
OILS, edible; OIL WELLS. In volume 3, under OIL,
they would find references to ASPHALT; CLAYS and
SHALES; COAL; GAS; WELLS and SPRINGS; as well as:
See also Vol. 7: OIL, MINERAL.

When each group has completed the task, points may be given for accuracy, amount of information and presentation. Each group could judge the other groups' results, give marks and one group would eventually win.

Another method of demonstrating the idea of topics and synonyms is for the librarian to have the class work out a 'subject index' for the school. Again the class can be split into groups, each group having one section or perhaps floor of the school. Each group would have to construct 'subject' headings on catalogue cards for the different people, departments and equipment in the school. Each heading would be followed by a Dewey number which the pupils would try to find out from the catalogue or by consulting, with the librarian, an abridged DEWEY DECIMAL CLASSIFICATION.

For example, the second floor may contain SCIENCE and headings for AQUARIUM, BIOLOGY, CHEMISTRY, LABORATORY, MICE, MICROSCOPES, PHYSICS, PLANTS etc would be necessary. On the ground floor headings might be needed for ADMINISTRATION, DINNER TICKETS, HEADMASTER, JANITOR, NURSE, PHOTO-COPIER, SECRETARY, TYPEWRITER etc. General headings covering different 'subjects' could be: FIRE ALARM: DOMESTIC SCIENCE or STOREROOM: BIOLOGY.

Discussions on what to include as headings would form a large part of this exercise or game. By debating whether DOMESTIC SCIENCE or HOME ECONOMICS (or both) is needed as a heading for that department or whether the head of school is the PRINCIPAL, RECTOR, HEADMASTER or HEAD TEACHER, will enable the pupils to have some realization of the breadth of seemingly specific topics and will help them in their approach to the catalogue.

Using the catalogue, like using a telephone and its directory, is a fairly simple process, once that process has been carefully explained. Lack of a careful, easily understood explanation, taking into account the difficulties pupils will face, may leave the pupils with the impression that the catalogue is a hindrance or barrier to library use. The librarian will be seeking to demonstrate, by examples at the catalogue and through library games, the ease with which the catalogue can be used and the effectiveness of the usage of the catalogue for information retrieval in the school library.

1. It is being assumed that the school library catalogue will consist of and author index, a classified index and a subject index. Librarians whose catalogues differ *in form* from this model, will have to adapt their explanations to the pupils. The basic principles of catalogue use will remain constant.
2. MARLAND, Michael: Responsibility for reading in the secondary school. SCHOOL LIBRARIAN volume 25, Number 2, June 1977, Page 108.
3. WINKWORTH, F.V.: User education in schools. British Library, 1977, Page 7.

Chapter Nine

Reference Material

The use of reference material in the school library and teaching pupils how to use this type of material, is a problem facing all librarians in schools. It is obvious that a library needs a reference section, consisting of atlases, dictionaries, yearbooks, encyclopaedias etc. to satisfy the random requests from staff or pupils for information which may not be found as quickly by consulting the library shelves.

In dealing with reference material, the librarian must ask the following questions.

1. Should the pupils be taught how to use reference works?
2. Should the mechanics of each type of reference work be explained the pupils by the librarian?
3. What effect will this type of instruction have on the pupils' image of reference works and their subsequent use of such works?

If the pupils are to use the library as a source of information and if that information is to be retrieved in as helpful a manner as possible, then pupils *will* need to be familiar with the layout and use of reference works.

In answering question 2 the librarian may return to chapter 2, where it is argued that one of the prerequisites of teaching library skills is that pupils have a need for the skills they are to be taught. With regard to the skills of the use of reference material, a distinction must be made. On the one hand, the pupils have a need for such skills. On the other hand, the pupils do *not* need to be taught these skills by the librarian. That is, it will be futile for the librarian to stand in front of the class and explain, either verbally or audio-visually, how a gazetteer or an atlas is used. The reason for this is that the explanation will be in isolation of the practical use of the reference work.

If the librarian explains the index in an atlas and then, as an example, says to the pupils 'Let's look up Wagga Wagga, in Australia', the pupils may well understand *how* the atlas in used, but may soon forget this. It will only be when the pupils are shown how, why and *in what context* an atlas is used, that they will appreciate its use.

Reference books may be compared to the tools in a car. The librarian can attend a series of lectures on car maintenance, where the use of every tool that is useful in a car is explained, in diagrams. Unless the librarian can then be shown the tools being used on a car, in response to certain circumstances, the previous explanations may be useless.

The solution to this problem may lie outside the library. Instead of the librarian teaching the use of individual reference works, the teachers of the different subjects could be encouraged to demonstrate the use of reference materials, in context. Thus the geography teacher could show the use of a gazetteer; the history teacher could explain how a dictionary of dates is used; and the science teacher could demonstrate the use of a chemistry handbook. The librarian's role would be to inform teachers of the existence of the various reference works and then perhaps lend a copy of each work to the teachers who could explain its use to different classes, at the appropriate time. The results may be twofold. Firstly the pupils would become familiar with the reference work and secondly, the teacher might direct pupils to the particular reference book at appropriate times.

On the other hand, the librarian may feel that, as the reference books will be used in the library, the use of such material should be taught in the library. The teaching should also be done in context if it is to be relevant to the pupils work. This implies, as with other library skills, that librarian—teacher cooperation is vital. The librarian's explanation of the use of a gazetteer, for example, must relate to the work done by pupils in their geography class. Thus it would be wasteful for the librarian to explain the different symbols in a gazetteer of Britain if the pupils were studying France in class. The symbols in a gazetteer of France might be the same, but the examples picked would be of no relevance to the pupils and this would affect their attitude to and understanding of the gazetteer.

General encyclopaedias (i.e. not encyclopaedias of specific topics e.g. encyclopaedia of birds) should be the province of the librarian. The librarian should take some time to explain the functions and use of encyclopaedias, because the encyclopaedias form a mini-library within the school library. If the school library is akin to a supermarket, then the encyclopaedias are akin to a general store. This analogy may be taken further by the librarian, by showing the pupils how, in a supermarket, a shopper could find not only a variety of goods, but also different brands of goods. In a general store, there may be the same variety of goods, but the shopper may discover that there is only one brand of each type of goods. So in the school library, a pupil seeking information on a particular topic will find a variety of books and non-book materials on that topic on the library shelves. In the encyclopaedias, the pupils will also find information on that topic, but in a very restricted form.

In explaining the use of the encyclopaedias, the librarian can show how the form of the encyclopaedias (alphabetical by subject) is similar to the major headings in the subject index. Also, it can be shown that the index to the encyclopaedias, usually contained in the last volume, is similar to the subject index, as a whole, in the school library catalogue. The process of finding information is also the same. The pupil will look up the subject in the encyclopaedia's index and will be given a number e.g. 10, (in bold type) 342. This indicates that the information required is on page 342 of volume 10. Thus another part of the library, the pupils can be shown, works in the same way as a telephone and telephone directory.

The librarian, in explaining the subject index in the school library catalogue, will have shown how the process does not always bring success if all the material on a particular topic has been borrowed by other readers. If this happens, the pupils should be encouraged to consult the subsidiary subject index, i.e. the encyclopaedias, so that they will always be able to find *some* information on most topics.

The librarian can show the pupils how and why they should use the encyclopaedias, but the librarian cannot, in isolation, instruct the pupils in the effective use of the encyclopaedias. There are often complaints that pupils doing projects merely copy out large sections of material from encyclopaedias. Proper use of the encyclopaedias in this context can only be done through the cooperation of the librarian and the teachers involved in supervising the projects.

The reference shelves in the school library should not merely be used for pupils looking at pictures (in an encyclopaedia of aeroplanes perhaps) but should represent a set of information tools which the pupils can use as aids to study, in the context of that study.

EXAMPLES

The use of reference material, especially encyclopaedias involves information skills and study skills. The most effective demonstration of the use of the encyclopaedias in the school library will be one which the pupils recognize as relevant to their needs. Thus the librarian can choose as an example a topic which the pupils have been studying in class on the same day as they visit the library.

A class may have been studying the human anatomy in biology and the librarian will be able to follow up this lesson, in cooperation with the biology teacher, by using the human anatomy as the topic to be looked for in the encyclopaedias. The librarian will be hoping to show the pupils how using the encyclopaedias involves a series of steps, like a train journey which involves changing trains or like a treasure hunt in which clues have to be followed in order to find the specific answer.

If we take the DIGESTIVE SYSTEM as the general topic looked for by one pupil and DUODENUM as the specific topic of another pupil, we can see how the librarian could demonstrate how the information is to be retrieved from the encyclopaedias.

In an encyclopaedia with a straight alphabetical sequence, such as the Children's Britannica,[2] the first pupil would look up DIGESTION in volume 6 and find the information required. If the second pupil consulted volume 6, he/she would not find DUODENUM because it is not listed as a separate heading. To find information on the DUODENUM, the pupil would have to follow the 'clues' given in the encyclopaedia.

Clue 1: DUODENUM is not in the alphabetical sequence, so consult the index.

Clue 2: DUODENUM is in the index.

Clue 3: DUODENUM can be found in volume 6, p.82

In the Oxford Junior Encyclopedia,[3] which is not in a straight alphabetical sequence, the pupil will have to consult the index to find:

DIGESTIVE SYSTEM, human: Vol. 11 – 104, 7, 140.

DIGESTIVE SYSTEM, animal: Vol. 2 – 194.

In this encyclopaedia, if the second pupil looks up DUODENUM, it will not be found in the index, so that this is a case where the pupil must widen the search to find a more general heading, i.e. DIGESTIVE SYSTEM. This is akin to a pupil wishing to go by train from town A to town B, but finding that there is no direct train. The pupil may then have to travel from town A into city C and out to town B.

The study skills will involve pupils in deciding what information they require. Do they want general information on the DIGESTIVE SYSTEM or do they want a drawing of the INTESTINE or a definition of the DUODENUM. The pupils can be shown how to look for sub-headings in the passage on the DIGESTIVE SYSTEM and how to pick out the relevant material. Also, if they come across words they do not understand, the pupils can be encouraged to seek an explanation in the encyclopaedias or to look up the words in a general dictionary. Pupils will also have to decide whether it is worthwhile following up the references given in the encyclopaedias. For example, do they need to look up ENDOCRINE GLANDS as is suggested in the passage on the DIGESTIVE SYSTEM.

The librarian may have to repeat these examples several times to some pupils. The pupils will learn by their own experience of the encyclopaedias but must first be shown, by direct example, how the encyclopaedias are to be properly exploited.

1. For the display aspects of teaching the use of encyclopaedias, see chapter eleven.
2. CHILDREN'S BRITANNICA. 20 volumes. 3rd edition, Encyclopaedia Britannica, 1973.
3. OXFORD JUNIOR ENCYCLOPEDIA. 23 volumes. O.U.P., 1964.

Chapter Ten

Display

The information skills which pupils are taught may not be easily remembered and the librarian must find a way of reinforcing these skills when the skills are most needed. Ideally, this would mean that each time a pupil used the catalogue or an encyclopaedia, the librarian would be on hand to explain the skills involved. This is obviously impractical, so the librarian has to devise a substitute for him/herself which will be permanently available to pupils. Thus 'display' in this chapter will mean not only the display of new books or books and materials on a particular topic, but all the notices, diagrams, reminders, posters and pictures which might be usefully pinned up around the library.

Pupils are accustomed to information being transmitted in notice form. They read numbers on a bus stop; notices on platforms in stations; instructions for seating in theatres, cinemas and football grounds; advertisements and guides in supermarkets; and technical instructions in telephone boxes, photographic booths and automatic ticket barriers. The display of instructions, guides and suggestions is a visual form of continuous teaching of library skills and, without causing confusion, the librarian should put up as many guides to library use as possible.

In the school library guidance to pupils should be ever-present. A pupil should never have to ask the librarian where the encyclopaedias are or need help to find his/her way around the shelves. Simple notices giving directions or shelf-guides can be made by using LETRASET[1] on white card. Even the most un-artistic librarian will be able to use LETRASET which is a series of letters and numbers on a sheet. When the sheet is placed on the card and the letters rubbed with the blunt end of a pencil, the letters are transmitted on to the card in a clear black colour which makes the words easy to read.

Using shelf-guides helps the pupil to use his/her library skills to the full. Thus if each shelf or every other shelf is labelled with a class number and the subject, the pupil will be able to follow the numbers more easily. For example, on the sports shelves one card would read.

796.33   FOOTBALL

On the fiction shelves letter guides would also help retrieval by the pupils and shelving by the librarian. It may also be helpful to put a piece of card on the side of each block of shelving, listing some of the subjects contained in those rows of shelves. The list can include broad topics as well as popular specific subjects. The list for the 600s might include:

610   MEDICINE
625   LOCOMOTIVES
629.13   FLIGHT
629.2   CARS

Such guides not only make the material easier to locate but take away some of the monotony of the shelves and attract the pupil's attention.

Notices in the library giving instructions to pupils who are using the catalogue or reference material are a vital back-up to teaching library skills. The notices must be prominent, legible and easily understood. It is worthwhile for the librarian to take some time in designing such notices which may become permanent fixtures in the library. Help on the design and layout of the notices should be sought if the librarian is in doubt. The instructions given must be understood by the average pupil and examples should be given, where possible.

The instructions for using the catalogue should be placed as close to the catalogue as possible, preferably above it, so that the pupil using the catalogue cannot fail to see the notice. The notice should tell the pupil how to locate material by author and by subject and what to do if the material cannot be found in the catalogue. As the subject approach to information may form the largest part of the pupil's school work, prominence should be given to this aspect of location. The notice might be as follows:

HOW TO USE THE CATALOGUE

1. If you know the author's name, look in the AUTHOR INDEX under his name.

CLASS NO.
598.2
J AM

JAMES, Edward

Birds of Britain. Batsford,
1973.

158p., illus.

The book can be found on the shelves at 598.2 JAM. Follow the numbers on the shelves until you come to 598.2 to find out if the book is there. If is out you may reserve it. If you have difficulty, ask the librarian.

2. If you want a book on a SUBJECT, look in the SUBJECT INDEX under the subject you want.

BIRDS   598.2

Go to the shelves to find out if there are any books on your subject. If you want to know all the material the library has on BIRDS, look in the CLASSIFIED CATALOGUE at 598.2

IF YOU HAVE ANY DIFFICULTY, ASK THE LIBRARIAN.

The librarian may feel that this notice is self-explanatory but the pupils may find it too long or too complicated. To offset such difficulties, the notice could be pinned up in two parts, side by side. The notice could also be accompanied by photographs at the side of the notice showing the various aspects of the catalogue and the catalogue card. For example, there might be an arrow from the explanation of the subject index to a photograph of a pupil using the subject index. Photographs of subject index cards showing different aspect of one subject might also be used. For example:

Photograph 1:   POLLUTION: CITIES   301.31
Photograph 2:   POLLUTION: NATURE   574.52

The photographs would create interest in the notice and break it up into easily understood sections. The last sentence is perhaps the most important. Getting pupils to ask for help in the school library (or any library) is a major task for the librarian. The pupils should be encouraged not to give up when they meet difficulties in retrieval.

Some pupils may have difficulty in successfully using reference material and it will be helpful if some visual guide can be devised to aid the pupils on the location of material in, for example, encyclopaedias. An example of such a guide might be a notice showing the use of an encyclopaedia for a topic and comparing its use to a bus or train journey. If we take CASTLES as our topic and use the OXFORD JUNIOR ENCYCLOPEDIA[2] as the reference book, the design of the notice can be seen.

What the librarian is attempting to point out in this display is how the use of the index of this encyclopaedia is similar to the use of a time-table in the bus-station in the town or city. Thus in an imaginary town the number 9 bus may go to MARCHMOUNT, the 31 to CROSSTOLL, the 44 to MURRAYGREEN and the 33 to TYNEHOUSE. Thus if a pupil wishes to go to MURRAYGREEN, he or she will have to find out, from the timetable, which bus goes there and at what time. If the pupil looks up CASTLES in the index of the OXFORD JUNIOR ENCYCLO-PEDIA, the following information is given.

CASTLES: X1-47; X-161
CASTLES, siege: X-410
CASTLES, upkeep of: X 266

In this case, volume eleven, page 47 will be the equivalent of the number 44 bus, at 2.30 pm. Volume ten page 161, will also give general information on CASTLES and is another route to the same destination. A diagram of the bus route in the locality of the school could be drawn up by the librarian and an equivalent diagram, for CASTLES and related subjects, could be used to demonstrate the use of the encyclopaedias. Such diagrams can again be accompanied by photographs of pupils using particular references in the encyclopaedia. A photographic sequence might be:

Picture 1:   The page showing CASTLES in the encyclopaedia
Picture 2:   A pupil following up a reference given on that page:
                 CRUSADES (Vol. 1) and picking out volume 1.

Picture 3:   Another pupil consulting the index to look up PALACES, a reference given under CASTLES.

Picture 4:   A pupil drawing a castle from a picture in the encyclopaedia.

The advantages of being such a visual display are that the librarian does not need to explain the use of the encyclopaedias to pupils each time they use the encyclopaedias. Also, photographs attract attention and remind the pupils of the existence of the encyclopaedias.

Other forms of display in the library may include work done by pupils. This will include book reviews and pictures drawn from a scene in a book which a pupil has read (see chapter 7). Posters, such as those obtainable from the National Book League[3] can also add to the library's attractiveness and help to interest the pupils.

The display of new books is perhaps the most traditional aspect of display in libraries and can be interesting and stimulating. Librarians should not be afraid, with the display of new books, to imitate the devices used in bookshops to attract the attention of book-buyers. There is no reason why, in the school library, 'The machine-gunners' by Robert Westall, should not be displayed as BOOK OF THE MONTH. A TOP TEN selection of books, fiction and non-fiction could also be displayed in the library.

In chapter seven it was suggested that WORLD WAR TWO might form a theme for presenting fiction to pupils. In displaying such material, the librarian can stimulate ideas within the pupil and also extend the pupil's library skills by demonstrating how material from different sections of the library can be used together. Such a display on World War Two might include some of the books mentioned in chapter seven, with book covers from other fiction books included, as a background to the display. Non-fiction material should also be displayed. A selection of material might include:

ELLIS, Keith:	Warriors and fighting men. (Gives the military aspects of World War Two as well as other wars in history)
HEALEY, Tim:	The Second World War (Chapters such as 'Inside Britain' show photographs of war-time Britain)
HOARE, Robert:	World War Two (Includes chapters on 'The home front' and 'Resistance and sabotage').
MOLLO, A.:	Naval, marine and air force uniforms of World War 2.
WORLD WAR TWO:	Slide set. (20 coloured slides showing different aspect of the war).[4]

In the display, the books should be opened up to show the wide range of topics covered. Fiction and non-fiction books can be linked, such as 'The silver sword' by Ian Serrailler and Robert Hoare,'World War Two'. If the librarian can project one or more of the slides, it will give more depth to the display. In addition to these commercially produced materials, the librarian can include in the display photographs taken in wartime of the pupils' grandparents or relatives; official papers, such as ration books which grandparents might still have; medals, caps, badges which have survived; model aeroplanes and tanks made by pupils; and records and tapes of war-time music and programmes. In mounting such a display the librarian will have to take care not to include too much material and also be security conscious in displaying the material brought in by pupils.

Such displays, mounted in the library or elsewhere in the school can promote the idea of subjects or topics having many different facets and may help the pupils in their own use of library materials. By including library displays outside the library and library information on notice boards, the librarian can take the library to the whole school. Pupils may even be encouraged to wear badges with a message such as: READ ON!

1. LETRASET is obtainable from library supplies and is produced by Letraset Ltd., 195 Waterloo Road, London.
2. OXFORD JUNIOR ENCYCLOPEDIA. 13 volumes. O.U.P., 1964.
3. ELLIS, Keith: Warriors and fighting men. Wayland, 1971.
    HEALEY, Tim: The Second World War. Macdonald, 1977.
    HOARE, Robert: World War Two: an illustrated history in colour 1939—1945. Macdonald, 1973.
    MOLLO, A.: Naval, marine and air force uniforms of World War Two. Blandford, 1973.
4. WORLD WAR TWO: Slide set. Slide Centre, 1972.

Chapter Eleven

Projects

Individual and group projects are becoming increasingly used as methods of learning in secondary schools as well as primary schools. Any subject inquiry in the school library, whether part of a project for a first year group or part of an assignment for a fifth year 'A' level pupil, can be grouped under 'project work'. Teaching library skills for project work, therefore includes training pupils to approach information by subject and it is this approach that pupils will most use in the school library.

Project or individual assignment work will start in the classroom, in the general teaching of the subject and it is from this base that the pupils will go to the school library to extend their knowledge of an individual topic. The library methods for this type of work should be taught as early as possible, preferably in the primary grades. Project work will involve the teacher and the librarian, who need to maintain close contacts so that the work done by individual pupils or by groups is closely monitored. (See chapter 4).

The library as a whole will be involved in this type of work and one of the concepts which the librarian will be trying to teach pupils is that of the library as a storehouse of information which comes in different forms. Information can be found in books, fiction and non-fiction, encyclopaedias and non-book materials and encouraging the pupils to use different but allied sources of information will be one of the librarian's aims.

If we take WATER as a topic for group/individual assignments we can see how the library can help in the pupils' search for information. Before the pupils reach the library however, they will have used study skills as a preliminary to their library work. Adequate teaching of study skills by teachers and librarians should ensure that the pupils have prepared their work prior to visiting the library. The pupils should know the purpose of their study and know, for example, whether they require information on WATER in general or on some specific aspect of the topic WATER, such as water in industry. They should also have a set of questions prepared, perhaps in cooperation with the class teacher, which can be answered in the library. Questions on WATER POLLUTION might include:

(1).   What are the main causes of water pollution?
(2).   Where are rivers most polluted?
(3).   What methods are used to clear water pollution?
(4).   What laws are there to prevent water pollution?

Co-operation between librarian and teacher will, indirectly, help pupils. If the librarian knows, *in advance*, of the topic being studied, material can be bought or borrowed; the librarian can check the adequacy of the catalogue entries (i.e. are the SUBJECT INDEX headings phrased in the language of the pupils?); the librarian and the teacher can discuss the study skills and information skills involved and decide whether any particular skills need re-inforcing; and, if necessary, workcards can be drawn up directing the pupils' search for information on WATER.

The pupils will firstly want to know what the school library has on their topic and will consult the SUBJECT INDEX. If they look under WATER, they may find several cards, covering different aspects of the topic. It is an important test of the pupils' grasp of library skills that they are able to appreciate that different aspects of the topic WATER will be in different parts of the library. As a person seeking the ingredients for a recipe will have to go to different parts of the supermarket for individual ingredients, so the pupils will have to consult material in different parts of the library to find information on the aspects of their topic. Thus if the pupils come to the library expecting all the material on all aspects of WATER to be on one shelf, then they have not appreciated the idea of classification by subject. When the introductory teaching of library skills has been successful, the pupils will be able to select the relevant headings they need and proceed from the SUBJECT INDEX to the shelves or to the CLASSIFIED CATALOGUE. In other words, they will be able to recognize the 'ingredients' needed to complete their 'recipe'.

The type of headings to be found in the SUBJECT INDEX might include:

WATER:	AGRICULTURE	631.7
WATER:	CHEMISTRY	546
WATER:	ECOLOGY	574.52
WATER:	ELECTRICITY	621.31
WATER:	GAMES	797.2
WATER:	HYGIENE	613
WATER:	IRRIGATION	631.7
WATER:	POWER	621.31
WATER:	RESOURCES	333.9
WATER:	SUPPLY SERVICES	350.81

Having found some of the material they require on the shelves, the pupils should then be able to appreciate the different sources of information contained in the library. This is especially relevant when, as may often happen, there is no specific material on a particular aspect of the topic to be found on the shelves. Thus if a pupil is seeking material on WATER in relation to PLANTS, the material on the shelves may be unavailable or inadequate. The pupil should then know to consult the reference works and encyclopaedias to find more information. Taking the pupils back to the supermarket analogy, it can be shown that if one of the ingredients on a recipe was PEAS, and none were available in the fresh vegetable section, the pupils could check in the frozen food section or the dried fruit and vegetable section to find the same ingredient.

A pupil who has understood the librarian's teaching of library skills will know that the SUBJECT INDEX number for WATER: PLANTS which may be 581.91, can be used as key to the reference shelves. Under the number 581 or 581.9 the pupil may find a reference work on BOTANY which will give details of the role of WATER in the growth of PLANTS.

The encyclopaedias will be the pupil's next source of information. How the pupil uses the encyclopaedias can demonstrate his/her attitude to the library as a whole. One of the results of learning library skills should be that the pupil carries information from one part of the library to another. Thus the pupil seeking information on WATER: PLANTS can use the headings in the library's SUBJECT INDEX as a basis for headings to look up in the encyclopaedias. For example, there may be a heading in the library's subject index for:

WATER: PONDLIFE   574.929

The pupil can then look up PONDLIFE, either in the straightforward alphabetical sequence in the encyclopaedia, or in the encyclopaedia's own subject index.

A second source of headings to look up in the encyclopaedias will arise from the material found on the shelves and in the CLASSIFIED CATALOGUE. In a general book on WATER, for example: 'Why we need water' by Mike Sanderson[1], the pupil will find some (but not much) information on:

Plants in the desert;
Plants in rain forests;
Plants that live in water;
Water and seeds;
Water and roots;
Measurement of water needed for plants;
Water and trees.

Having found these possible headings, the pupil can consult the encyclopaedias for further information. In the Oxford Junior Encyclopedia, headings in the index include:

PLANT BREEDING:	Vol. 6 — 336
PLANTS: desert:	Vol. 2 — 118
PLANTS: pond:	Vol. 2 — 460
PLANTS: nutrition:	Vol. 2 — 294
PLANTS: water:	Vol. 2 — 294
SEEDS: fertilization:	Vol. 6 — 150
WATERCRESS:	Vol. 6 — 477
WATER GARDENS:	Vol. 6 — 478
WATER LILY:	Vol. 13 — 64
WATER: plants:	Vol. 2 — 458

The ability of the pupils to present the information they have found in the library in an organized form, will depend on how well they have learned the necessary study skills but it will always be helpful for the pupils to be given reminders of the skills involved by the teacher or the librarian when the pupils are completing their assignments in the library. Help can be given to pupils in bringing together and comparing information found in books, encyclopaedias, slide-sets etc., so that they produce work which is not merely a copied-out tract from an encyclopaedia. It may be better for the work done by pupils to be structured by the use of work cards or sets of questions to be answered which can be drawn up by the teacher and librarian, until the pupils have had sufficient practice to be able to cope with the retrieval of information by themselves. If both the teacher and librarian are involved in the production of workcards, the pupils can be helped in their search for information and also in the type of information they require.

The success or otherwise of projects based on library materials should be discussed by the librarian and the teacher to evaluate the effects of teaching library skills to the pupils and to discover if the desired effect of teaching such skills, more effective use of library materials by pupils, has been achieved. Evaluation by the librarian and the teacher may result in the librarian ordering more material on an aspect of the topic WATER which the pupils found either difficult to understand or which was insufficiently covered by the existing material in the library. The librarian may have found that the pupils' understanding of the terminology of the topic was not adequate and that this affected their use of the catalogue and encyclopaedias. By (tactfully) informing the teacher of this problem, mistakes can be avoided in future projects. The greater the discussion of this type of problem by librarian and teacher, the more pupils will ultimately benefit.

1. Materials in the school library on WATER might include:-
   HENRY, Bernard: Water. Baker, 1968.
   HEYERDAHL, T.: Waters of the world. Tape cassette, Seminar, 1972.
   JACKMAN, L: Exploring the pond. Evans, 1976.
   SANDERSON, M.: Why we need water. Macdonald, 1977.
   SOWRY, J.: Water. Priory Press, 1976.
   THOMPSON, L.: The story of water. Macmillan, 1974.
   The water in your tap: Slide set, Hunter, 1974.
   The world of water: Slide set, Slide Centre, 1970.

Chapter Twelve

Evaluation

Having taught the pupils the skills needed to use the school library effectively, the librarian cannot sit back and expect that the pupils will automatically become expert library users. Teaching library skills will be a never ending part of a librarian's role in the school. Having taught the skills formally and *collectively* (i.e. to classes or groups of children) the librarian will have to reinforce this teaching by attempting to solve the *individual* difficulties which pupils may face when using the library.

This may be seen as a form of continuous evaluation of how the pupils put their library skills into practice. Having taught the library skills to pupils, the librarian may feel that there must be an immediate evaluation of how the pupils have understood the implications of the various skills. This evaluation, however, need not follow the kind of assessment done in the classroom, so that setting a question paper on, for example, the use of the catalogue, may be worthless. This will be because the nature of the examination will not be relevant to the skills being taught. The pupils will need to know how to use the catalogue but they do not need to be able to express their actions in words. A question such as: 'Why whould you use the subject index?' may only prove the pupils' grasp of or lack of the terminology of librarianship, rather than their understanding of the mechanics of the subject index.

Another type of evaluation done in some school libraries consists of the use of commercially produced workcards or textbooks. In this type of material, pupils are given various assignments to be completed in the school library, such as:

(1) What is meant by Daylight Saving?
(2) Who first thought of changing the clocks?

This type of example, taken from a set of questions designed to make pupils use an encyclopaedia[1] will be irrelevant to the pupils, unless they happen to be doing a project on that particular topic. This is not to say that *all* workcards are irrelevant. If the librarian, in consultation with the pupils' class teachers, can draw up workcards which relate directly to the pupils' curricular work, then the completion of the workcards and the use of the library in doing so, will represent to the pupils a logical extension of their school work. The library will appear more relevant to the rest of their school activities. The danger in using commercially produced workcards or textbooks is that the pupils will see the evaluation as just another test in a particular subject, in this case 'library'. The library should not become another subject department in the minds of the pupils.

When skills of various kinds are taught in schools, teachers carefully prepare the teaching of such skills and there is usually a large amount of repetition by the teacher of the skills involved, because the pupils cannot assimilate new skills immediately. This is particularly true of library skills and librarians should be aware that library skills, for most pupils, will need to be taught over and over again, *when the skills are needed*. As each individual pupil uses the library and faces difficulties, the librarian and the teachers will have to be prepared to explain, in context, the different library skills involved. When parents are teaching their children how and where to cross the road (at a Pelican Crossing, for example) they do not merely take the child once to the crossing, explain the sequence of lights and leave the child to remember their instructions. The skills involved are repeated each time the child has to cross the road at that crossing. Thus in the school library, when pupils use the catalogue, they may need assistance from the librarian or teacher and will only learn how to use the catalogue effectively by experience, with the help of repeated instructions, at the point of need.

The development of teaching methods which involve the pupils in individual learning experiences has seen the growth of topic or project work. When the pupils use the library for this type of work, the librarian, cooperating with the class teacher or group of teachers, can carry out continuous evaluation of library skills. Also, before setting projects for individual pupils or groups of pupils, the librarian can quickly indicate, as an introduction to the particular project, the way in which the pupils should exploit the library's resources. In this way, the pupils will recognize the use of the library as an essential part of project work and will look upon the librarian's introductory talk as a normal part of every project. The librarian will use examples from the particular project under discussion, thereby immediately relating the library skills to the needs of the pupils.

In some schools[2] the use made by the pupils of the school library is done mainly in library periods which are timetabled in the same way as other subjects. These library periods can be made to be extremely helpful to both pupils and teacher, if they are properly organized by the librarian and the teacher. If they are used well, these periods can be an ideal time to evaluate the pupils' use of the library, especially if the time is used for work which is directly related to the pupils' curricular activities.

Library periods, however, are often abused and it is from the misuse of such time that antiquated ideas of the school library are perpetuated. An example of this misuse is when pupils are taken to the library and forced to read a book (any book) for forty minutes. The logic behind this method of library use is that books are good for children and if the teacher can maintain silence in the library for a period, then the pupils will benefit in some way. What actually occurs in such a situation is that many pupils do not read the books they are given and they gain an image of the school library, as a place in the school, separate from the school itself, where pupils are forced to engage in an activity which is of no relevance to other school work.

A more constructive use of the school library is one which does not include timetabled library periods, but which regards the library as an integral part of all subjects taught in the school. This implies that the library will be open for use by individual pupils at all times and for classes or groups of pupils, at times suitable to the work being done by particular classes. A teacher may then plan his/her course in advance and reserve a time when the library can be used by the class, *for a specific purpose*. Library skills can then be evaluated (and repeated if necessary) when they are most needed.

The evaluation of library skills will be necessary for pupils, teachers and librarians, so that by resolving difficulties faced in using the library, greater and more effective use of the school library can be achieved.

EXAMPLES

The following is an example of the type of questions which could be asked on a workcard given to pupils. It must be stressed again that such a workcard would only be given as a direct consequence of what pupils were studying in school. If the pupils were studying local government as part of a social education programme, they could be asked to use the library for part of their studies, to widen their knowledge of the subject. The workcards would *follow* the teaching of the topic, so that pupils would be aware of the terminology involved in the study of local government. This would ensure that the pupils would view their library based work as part of their educational studies and not merely as an exercise to test their library skills. The workcards would only be given to pupils who had been taught library skills previously.

LOCAL GOVERNMENT

A. (1). The number in the SUBJECT INDEX for LOCAL GOVERN-MENT is:

(2). Write down the author and title of two books in the CLASSI-FIED INDEX on LOCAL GOVERNMENT
(a).
(b).

(3). Write down the author and title of two books you found on the shelves on LOCAL GOVERNMENT.
(a).
(b).

(4). Are there any non-book materials (films, cassettes, kits etc) listed in the CLASSIFIED INDEX on LOCAL GOVERNMENT.

B. The departments of local government include HEALTH, LEISURE, EDUCATION and PUBLIC UTILITIES.
What headings could you look up in the SUBJECT INDEX for information on the following department.

(1). *HEALTH*
(a).
(b).

(2). *LEISURE*
(a).
(b).

(3). *EDUCATION*
    (a).
    (b).

(4). *PUBLIC UTILITIES.*
    (a).
    (b).

(5). Write down 2 books (or non-book materials) in the CLASSI-
FIED INDEX from 1, 2, 3, or 4.

C. (1). What headings could you look up in the encyclopaedia for
information on SOCIAL SERVICES.
    (a).
    (b).

(2). Which reference works could you use for more information on
SOCIAL SERVICES.
    (a).
    (b).

D. List three publications by different departments in X city or town.
    (a).
    (b).
    (c).

Where can these books be found on the shelves.
    (a).
    (b).
    (c).

1. HOWARD, M.: Library assignments. 2nd edition, Arnold, 1968. Page 9.
2. Library periods are still used extensively in secondary schools in Great Britain
but less so in the United States and Australia. The employment of full-time
school librarians is one cause of the move away from time-tabled library
periods.

Chapter Thirteen

Conclusion

If the premises set out in this book, that pupils need to be taught library skills in order that they may use the school library effectively, is accepted, then there are several implications which must be considered.

In chapter one, it was stated that a prime aim of teaching library skills was to enable pupils to become 'competent library users'. A competent library user should be able to put into practice the library skills taught by the librarian. Such a pupil will understand the organization of the library; the retrieval system operated in the library; the range of materials, both books and non-book materials, available in the library; the uses of reference material; the types and range of fiction available. In short, this pupil will be able to use the school library according to his/her needs at any one time, whether the need is for a work of fiction for light reading or for detailed information, in print or audio-visual form, on a particular topic. By implication, a pupil competent in the school library will generally be competent in a public library or another educational library, although this will depend on the system operated in any one library. A pupil who has grasped the idea of how libraries are organized and how information is generally found, should be competent in any library.

It can be argued, with some justification, that as soon as pupils can read, they should be introduced to library skills in a limited form. For example, the books in a primary school classroom could be classified by the first figure of the Dewey main classes. Thus all books on science would be labelled 5 and history books 9. Such a scheme would introduce the idea of classification to pupils at an early age. If pupils are expected to use library skills of an advanced order in secondary schools, then by implication, they will need to have been taught some library skills in the primary school. A structure for library skills can be worked out in a primary school so that pupils progress from the classroom library to the school library, gradually learning more complicated skills as they become older.

Thus a classroom library for 8–9 year olds may have books classified by the first two figures of the Dewey number, which will enable the books on NATURE, for example, to be separated from the general science books. It may also be possible to construct a simplified catalogue or subject index, made by the pupils themselves, to introduce elements of retrieval. When the pupils use the primary school library, help can be given to all grades by the lettering on the books and non-book materials. Thus a boxed cassette on NATURE may have on its spine a large 5 (for early grades), a smaller 7 (57 for intermediate grades) and a smaller 4 (574 for top grades, aged 10–11). This type of gradual introduction to library techniques and concepts will help pupils become accustomed to libraries, so that when they reach the secondary school, they will not be intimidated by the larger size of the secondary school library.

Having argued that library skills should be a part of primary education implies a knowledge of libraries and library skills on the part of primary school teachers which may not always exist. For example, the study skills required to use material effectively may be taught in primary schools and pupils may be able to be selective in their reading of material or may be able to skim material to extract the relevant information. On the other hand, the skills may never be taught in connection with library use or the pupils may be left unaware of the direct connection between study skills and information skills.

It is important, therefore, that primary school teachers be able to teach both basic information skills and study skills, so that pupils can carry these skills into secondary school. This implies that library skills should be part of the courses taken by primary teachers in colleges of education. The library element of courses on reading development, children's literature and general teaching methods should be introduced or increased, so that primary teachers become aware of the importance of library skills and their connection with other skills taught in primary schools. A further implication for colleges of education is that more teaching may have to be done by librarians and more staff may be needed for library duties.

The implication of teaching library skills effectively for the staffing of school libraries is that the skills can only be fully taught by a full-time school librarian. A teacher-librarian with only part of his/her timetable for library work could not hope to organize and help to teach the introductory sessions on library skills and follow this up with the repetitions of the skills involved for individual and group assignments. In America, Canada and Australia, school librarians are the norm for secondary schools but in Britain the widespread appointment of school librarians has been confined to enlightened areas of the country such as Inner London, Nottinghamshire, Cheshire, Lanarkshire and Stirlingshire. Most schools still do not have full-time librarians. If library skills are seen as necessary to the pupils' learning in schools and as corollaries to modern teaching methods, then more school librarians are urgently needed.

Assuming the presence of a school librarian with the time, willingness and ability to teach library skills, the pupils will become more adept at using the school library. Teaching library skills will increase the pupils' awareness not only of what material the library has, but also what it lacks. The increase in demand for the existing material will be marked when more pupils become aware of the material. It follows that the budgets allocated to school libraries, in Britain at least, will have to be increased as more money will be needed to ensure that sufficient material is available for pupils and staff engaging in individual or group work or seeking fiction books or recreational reading. Teaching library skills in a poorly equipped and poorly stocked library can only lead to frustration and disappointment on the part of the pupils.

The services provided by local authorities for school libraries also need to be improved in many areas in Britain, so that school librarians have adequate borrowing facilities from a central bank of resources (such as the Bell Educational Resource Centre in Lanarkshire) to support work done in the school. For example, a project on the local environment may require material which the school library has not obtained or cannot afford. A well-equipped (in materials and staff expertise) schools library service can often ensure the success of such projects.

Even a well-equipped, well-stocked, well-staffed, well-supported school library, with a librarian who teaches library skills, will not be completely successful without the support of the teaching staff in the school. The staff will only be actively involved in the school library if they appreciate the use of the library; understand the library system and the skills taught to pupils; and appreciate the value of the library for their own particular subject. This implies that there is a need for either courses at college on school libraries or for inservice training within the school library resource centre for teachers in a particular

school. Teaching the teachers about school libraries is a difficult hurdle
for librarians to cross, but a vital one.

Teaching library skills affects not only pupils but librarians and
teachers. Only a combination of effort by all three will produce school
libraries which are the educational centres of modern schools.

Bibliography

BESWICK, Norman, (1977). *Resource-based learning.* Heinemann Educational.

GRIMSHAW, Ernest, (1952). *The teacher-librarian.* Arnold.

HART, W.J. Towards a philosophy of school libraries. *School Librarian* Vol. 17 No. 2. June 1969.

HERRING, J.E. Is seeing believing? Library skills and the audiovisual librarian. *The Audiovisual Librarian,* Vol. 4, no. 4 Autumn 1978.

HOWARD, M. (1968). *Library assignments.* 2nd edition. Arnold.

LINDSAY, John. Information training in secondary schools. *Educational Libraries Bulletin,* No. 57, Autumn, 1976.

MARLAND, Michael Responsibility for reading in the secondary school. *School Librarian.* Vol. 25 No. 2. June 1977.

OPEN UNIVERSITY: (1973). PE261. *Reading development, units 3 and 4.* Open University Press.

POLETTE, Nancy (1973). *Developing methods of inquiry.* USA, Scarecrow Press.

ROE, Ernest (1965). *Teachers, librarians and children.* Crosby Lockwood.

SAUNDERS, Helen E. (1968). *The modern school library: its administration as a materials center.* USA, Scarecrow Press.

SCHOOL LIBRARY ASSOCIATION. (1972). *Libraries in secondary schools,* edited by C.W. Morris, A.B. Russell, C. A. Stott. School Library Association.

SCHOOLS COUNCIL. Working Paper 43. (1972). School resource centres: the report of the first year of the Schools Council Resource Centre Project, by Norman Beswick. Evans/Methuen for the Schools Council.

SMITH, Barbara G. How do I join please? *School Librarian.* Vol. 24 No. 2 June 1976.

WINKWORTH, F.V.: (1977). *User education in schools.* British Library.

Index